GROUNDBREAKER
CRABTREE
BIOGRAPHIES

Elie Wiesel

HOLOCAUST SURVIVOR
AND MESSENGER FOR HUMANITY

By Diane Dakers

Crabtree Publishing Company
www.crabtreebooks.com

Author: Diane Dakers
Publishing plan research and development:
  Sean Charlebois, Reagan Miller
  Crabtree Publishing Company
Editors: Mark Sachner, Lynn Peppas
Proofreader: Rachel Eagen
Indexer: Ruth Owen
Editorial director: Kathy Middleton
Photo researcher: Mark Sachner
Designer: Alix Wood
Production coordinator: Margaret Amy Salter
Prepress technician: Margaret Amy Salter
Print coordinator: Katherine Berti

Written, developed, and produced by Water Buffalo Books

Publisher's note:
All quotations in this book come from original sources and contain the spelling and grammatical inconsistencies of the original text. The use of such constructions is for the sake of preserving the historical and literary accuracy of the sources.

Cover: Since his liberation near the end of World War II from Buchenwald, a Nazi concentration camp, Elie Wiesel has led an accomplished life as a writer, university professor, and political activist. Over his lifetime, he has devoted himself to speaking out against oppression, racism, and human suffering around the world. This photo, taken in 1945, shows the young Elie (face circled) with other Jewish slave laborers at Buchenwald, where ill-fed, poorly clothed inmates were crowded into narrow bunks.

Photographs and reproductions:
Corbis: Van Parys Media/Sygma: page 1; LGI Stock: page 77; Chip East: page 96; Chip East: page 97; Michael Kappeler/Pool/epa: page 102
Creative Commons (Wikipedia): David Shankbone: front cover (left), page 103 (main); Elie Wiesel: page 4 (inset), page 9, page 103 (inset); Veni Markovski: pages 5, 15 (right), 33, 55, 73, 87; Bundesarchiv: pages 12, 18, 22, 26, 27, 34, 42, 43, 44, 46, 47, 56, 57, 80 (left); 90 (second from bottom), 94, 95, 101; Daniel Ullrich, Three Dots: pages 13 (top right), 38 (top), 90 (top); Kitkatcrazy: pages 13 (second from top right), 38 (second from top), 90 (second from top); page 13 (second from bottom right); page 38 (second from bottom); The devious diesel: pages 13 (bottom right), 38 (bottom), 90 (bottom); page 19; page 23 (bottom); page 24; page 48; page 59 (middle left); page 64; page 66; page 69; page 79; page 81; page 95; page 96 (left); page 97 (right)
Getty Images: Philippe Wojazer: page 13 (bottom left); CBS Photo Archive: page 70; Keystone-France: page 75; Richard Wells: page 82; Sven Nackstrand: page 90
Public domain: front cover (right); page 4 (background); page 6; page 8; page 10; page 11; page 15; page 16; page 25; page 30; page 31; page 35; page 36; page 39; page 40; page 41 (left); page 49; page 51; page 53; page 56; page 57; page 58; page 59 (top left); page 59 (middle right); page 59 (bottom right); page 60; page 61; page 62; page 64 (left); page 65 (left); page 65 (right); page 68; page 80 (right); page 84; page 88; page 92 (both); page 93; page 99
Shutterstock: page 23 (top); page 29; page 41 (right); page 45; page 67; page 83

Library and Archives Canada Cataloguing in Publication

Dakers, Diane
    Elie Wiesel : Holocaust survivor and messenger for humanity / Diane Dakers.

(Crabtree groundbreaker biographies)
Includes index.
Issued also in electronic formats.
ISBN 978-0-7787-2552-7 (bound).--ISBN 978-0-7787-2555-8 (pbk.)

    1. Wiesel, Elie, 1928- --Juvenile literature. 2. Authors, French--20th century--Biography--Juvenile literature. 3. Jewish authors--Biography--Juvenile literature. 4. Holocaust survivors--Biography--Juvenile literature. I. Title. II. Series: Crabtree groundbreaker biographies

PQ2683.I33Z65 2012   j843'.914   C2012-901518-0

Library of Congress Cataloging-in-Publication Data

Dakers, Diane.
  Elie Wiesel : Holocaust survivor and messenger for humanity / Diane Dakers.
      p. cm. -- (Crabtree groundbreaker biographies)
  Includes index.
  ISBN 978-0-7787-2552-7 (reinforced library binding : alk. paper) -- ISBN 978-0-7787-2555-8 (pbk. : alk. paper) -- ISBN 978-1-4271-7860-2 (electronic pdf) -- ISBN 978-1-4271-7975-3 (electronic html)
  1. Wiesel, Elie, 1928---Juvenile literature. I. Title.

PQ2683.I32Z654 2012
813'.54--dc23
[B]
                                           2012008273

Crabtree Publishing Company

www.crabtreebooks.com   1-800-387-7650

Printed in the U.S.A./012014/SN20131105

Published in Canada
Crabtree Publishing
616 Welland Ave.
St. Catharines, ON
L2M 5V6

Published in the United States
Crabtree Publishing
PMB 59051
350 Fifth Avenue, 59th Floor
New York, New York 10118

Published in the United Kingdom
Crabtree Publishing
Maritime House
Basin Road North, Hove
BN41 1WR

Published in Australia
Crabtree Publishing
3 Charles Street
Coburg North
VIC, 3058

Contents

Chapter 1
Breaking Free from Silence

Early in his journalism career, Elie Wiesel made an appointment to interview famous French writer and Nobel Prize winner François Mauriac. Mauriac, who was Catholic, kept bringing the conversation back to one of his favorite subjects—the suffering of Jesus. Elie kept trying, unsuccessfully, to bring the conversation back to other topics. Finally, frustrated and overcome with emotion, he burst out that ten years earlier, during World War II, he had seen "hundreds of Jewish children, who suffered more than Jesus did on his cross." He then fled the room, humiliated by his outburst.

A Writing Career Begins

Mauriac ran after the young man and asked him what was wrong. Elie then confided that he had been one of those Jewish children, that he had been forced from his home and transported on a crowded train to a German concentration camp called Auschwitz.

Elie poured out his memories to Mauriac. As he did, the elder writer told the 26-year-old he must tell his story, he must write it down, so others would know the horrific things Elie—and millions of other Jews—had experienced at the hands of Nazi Germany during World War II.

Opposite: Elie Wiesel with his wife, Marion Wiesel, in 1989. Elie has done most of his writing in three languages—Yiddish, French, and English. Marion, an accomplished author in her own right, has been his translator for many years.

Inset: Elie in 1943 or 1944, at the age of 15.

WORLD WAR II: A BRIEF SKETCH

On September 1, 1939, the military forces of Nazi Germany, led by Adolf Hitler, invaded Poland. Within days, Poland, Britain, France, Canada, Australia, New Zealand, India, and South Africa declared war on Germany.

That was the beginning of World War II, which lasted in Europe until Germany surrendered on May 7, 1945. The war in Asia continued until Japan—which sided with Germany—formally surrendered on September 2, 1945. During that time, almost every country in the world became involved in the conflict. If a country sided with Germany, it was part of the so-called "Axis." If a country sided with Britain and France—the two major powers first to declare war on Germany—it was one of the "Allies."

The main Axis nations were Germany, Italy, Japan, Hungary, and Romania. The Allies initially consisted of the countries that had immediately declared war on Germany. Over the next few years, most of the world's nations joined the Allies. The largest Allied nations—the Soviet Union (now Russia), the United States, and China—joined the fight in 1941. A year later, 26 Allied countries formed the United Nations. (After the war, another 25 countries joined the UN.)

In Europe, Nazi Germany was highly successful in its efforts to invade and take over countries in all directions. By 1943, the Nazis had increased their territory to include most of continental Europe as we know it today. They made a big mistake, though, when they started moving into the Soviet Union in 1941.

U.S. soldiers pose with a Nazi flag captured during the assault on German forces in France by U.S., British, and Canadian troops in 1944.

At the start of the war, while Germany was moving into Eastern Europe from the west, the Soviet Union was moving in from the east. The two military powers agreed at that time not to challenge each other's territory. When Germany broke that agreement and started invading Soviet-held areas, the Soviet Union joined the Allies in fighting against Germany. That significantly increased the number of forces opposing the Nazi military.

Meanwhile, in Asia, Japan had invaded Manchuria (now northeast China) in 1931, and China in 1937. After World War II started in Europe, Japan joined the Axis, siding with Germany. To try to prevent Japan from dominating Asia, the United States stopped all trade with Japan. The most significant thing the United States did was stop selling oil to Japan, potentially crippling the Japanese military.

In return, to make sure the United States didn't become the dominant force in the Pacific, Japan bombed Pearl Harbor, Hawaii, on December 7, 1941. Japan also formally declared war on the United States. That led Britain, Canada, and the United States to declare war on Japan. Germany and Italy then declared war on the United States, and the United States declared war on those two nations.

Over the next few years, as the Soviets attacked Germany from the east, other Allied forces—Britain, Canada, and the United States, among others—attacked from the west and south, eventually beating the Germans into surrender. Adolf Hitler committed suicide on April 30, 1945. Germany surrendered a week later, marking the end of World War II in Europe.

At the same time, Japan was battling the Allies over Asian land and Pacific islands. Each side won individual battles—until August 6, 1945. That's the day the U.S. Air Force dropped an atomic bomb on Hiroshima, Japan. Three days later, the United States dropped another atomic bomb on another Japanese city, Nagasaki. More than 120,000 civilians died because of those bombs—either during the bombing or from radiation exposure after the bombing.

Within days of the bombings, Japan agreed to surrender to the Allies, and on September 2, 1945, World War II was officially over in the Pacific.

World War II was the biggest war in history. About 100 million military personnel fought in the war, and 50 to 70 million civilians, or non-military people, died, making it the deadliest war in history. It was also the only war to use nuclear weapons.

A Beginning and an End to Silence

When Elie, his family, and all their Jewish
neighbors were forcibly taken from their homes
in Romania, he was just 15 years old. As soon
as they arrived at Auschwitz, guarded by
attack dogs and soldiers with machine guns,
Elie and his father, Shlomo, were separated
from his mother and sisters. Elie would
never see his mother, Sarah, or his little
sister, Tzipora, again.

For almost a year, Elie and his father
managed to stay together, as they were moved

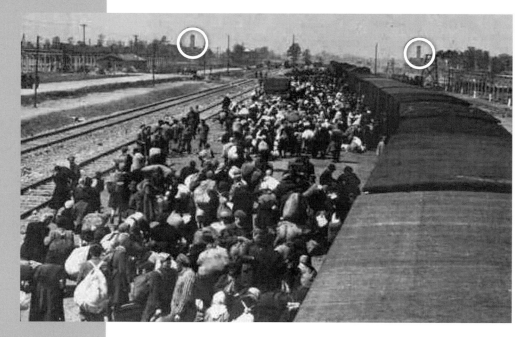

*Jews from a region of Eastern Europe near Elie
Wiesel's home village are shown being taken off of
trains at Auschwitz in 1944. Most of those who
weren't used for slave labor or medical experiments
were killed in gas chambers hours after their
arrival. The chambers were located in the
basements of the crematories, where the bodies
were burned (chimneys circled in background).*

Elie vowed he would not speak or write of these experiences for at least ten years.

Elie Wiesel and his father, Shlomo (shown here), stayed together through most of the time Elie was in the concentration camps of World War II. The experiences they shared shaped Elie's life and work for decades following Shlomo's death and Elie's release from Buchenwald.

from concentration camp to concentration camp. They were tortured, starved, and forced to work as slave laborers. They watched as fellow inmates were shot, hanged, or beaten to death. They lived in filthy conditions with no soap, clean water, or toilet facilities. Elie barely survived; Shlomo did not make it.

After he was liberated from Buchenwald concentration camp in 1945, Elie vowed he would not speak or write of these experiences for at least ten years. "I knew that, while I had many things to say, I did not have the words to say them," he wrote years later.

He felt he needed a decade for the right words to come to him, to be able to explain something that could not be explained to those who had not lived through it.

By the time Elie met with François Mauriac in Paris, the ten years he had vowed to remain silent had passed. So, with the elder man's encouragement, he started to write.

Over the next year he penned the manuscript for his first book. It was first published in the Yiddish language. It was later translated and published in French, and finally, in English in 1960, as *Night*.

THE HOLOCAUST: A STAIN ON THE FACE OF HUMANITY

Under the leadership of Adolf Hitler, the Nazi Party promoted the idea of one group that was superior to all others—a "master race" made up of people of northern European descent. Members of this group, called "Aryans" in Nazi propaganda, were set off against other groups.

Before World War II began, the Nazis began to make life difficult for Jews in Germany, enforcing curfews and creating discriminatory laws. It wasn't until World War II began in 1939, however, that Hitler made clear his ultimate goal—what later became known as the "Final Solution"—the organized mass murder, or genocide, of all the Jews in Europe.

In the early years of the war, the Nazis packed Jews into crowded, unsanitary ghettos in German-occupied Poland and parts of the Soviet Union. The most brutal of these ghettos were walled off or surrounded by barbed wire, and hundreds of thousands of occupants died of disease and starvation. In some ghettos, the occupants organized uprisings against the Nazis. All of them failed, and most of those involved in the uprisings were killed.

By the end of the war, most of the ghettos had been liquidated, or destroyed. Their residents were killed outright or removed by force to concentration camps. There, people died by many means. Many were

In this photograph, taken in 1942, German soldiers are shown executing Jews from Kiev, Ukraine (then part of the Soviet Union). The victims include a man trying to protect his child. The soldiers are members of a German mobile army killing unit.

starved or worked to death, shot by firing squads, or killed in massive gas chambers following "selections" in which people were chosen to live as slaves or die.

The Nazis singled out European Jews as the primary targets of their campaigns of threats, deportation, and slaughter. They also persecuted and murdered members of other groups on the basis of race, nationality, religion, or politics. People were targeted on the basis of whatever branded them as a threat to the Nazis' false standards of racial and political superiority.

By the end of the war, approximately six million Jews had been killed, along with millions of others, by the Nazis, other Axis nations, and those who cooperated, or collaborated, with them. Many years after the war, the organized, government-authorized extermination of Jews became known as the *Holocaust*. The word is of Greek origin, meaning "sacrifice by fire." The term has also, over time, become broadened to include other civilians who were selectively chosen by the Nazis for slaughter.

In one of the best-known photographs of World War II, a group of Jews is rounded up during the liquidation, or destruction, of the Warsaw Ghetto following the failed uprising of 1943.

"In spite of everything, what human beings have done to my people, and to other human beings, I believe in the humanity of the human being. I have problems with God. That's because I believe in God. If I stopped believing in God, I would have no problems."

Elie Wiesel, 2007

As a memoir, *Night* details Elie's Holocaust experiences. It also outlines his conflicted relationship with God, as the horrors at Auschwitz called into question the loving Creator he had worshiped during his deeply religious childhood.

Even though Elie has since written 50 more books, *Night* is still the one he considers his most significant—and the rest of the world seems to agree. The book has been translated into 30 languages. It is used as required reading in many high schools and colleges, and it has sold millions of copies around the globe. Elie gets about 100 letters a month from children who have read *Night*.

Over his lifetime, Elie has earned dozens of literary awards for his books, but in addition to writing, he has devoted his life to speaking out against oppression, racism, and human suffering around the world. In 1986, Elie was awarded the Nobel Peace Prize and honored, in the words of the Norwegian Nobel Committee, as "a messenger to mankind" and "a human being dedicated to humanity."

Elie has also earned some of the highest honors one can receive from nations around the world. These honors include the U.S.

Congressional Gold Medal of Achievement and the Presidential Medal of Freedom, entry into the French Legion of Honor, and an honorary knighthood from England's Queen Elizabeth II.

A university professor, in-demand speaker, and political activist who now makes his home in New York City, Elie Wiesel has advised U.S. presidents from Jimmy Carter to Barack Obama. He is an advocate for peace who counts the Dalai Lama among his friends. He is also a haunted survivor who doesn't want to remember his terrible wartime experiences— but refuses to let anyone forget.

Elie Wiesel's work, words, and wisdom are celebrated around the globe. In a sense, he has become a citizen of the world. But his life didn't start with such wide horizons. As a boy, he lived in a small, isolated town in Eastern Europe, where his family and religious studies were his entire world.

Elie Wiesel is awarded entry into the Legion of Honor by President François Mitterand of France in Paris, in 1984.

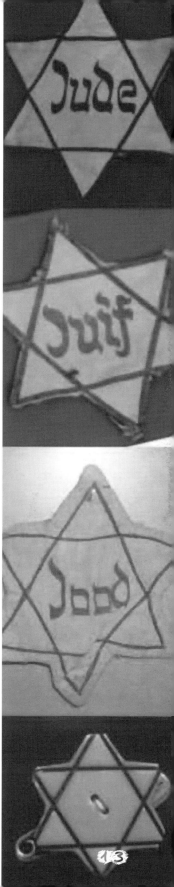

Chapter 2
Early Life and Education

Born in Sighet, a town in the historical region of Transylvania, Romania, on September 30, 1928, Eliezer ("Elie") Wiesel was the third of four children—the only son—born to a respected, well-to-do merchant and his wife. The family lived in a shtetl, or Jewish district, within Sighet, a town in the Carpathian Mountains that had been the hub of the region's Jewish community for 300 years.

Family Life

Elie's father, Shlomo, owned a grocery store, where his mother, Sarah, and elder sisters Hilda and Bea often helped out. Elie, on the other hand, could usually be found with his

The house in Sighet, Romania, where Elie Wiesel was born, photographed in 2007.

KABBALAH

Kabbalah is an ancient, mystical branch of the Jewish faith that seeks to explain the connection between a single Creator and human beings. The Creator has infinite, or limitless, wisdom, but humans have limits in their ability to understand. Followers of Kabbalah, therefore, try to understand the Creator's *limitless* universe to the best of their *limited* abilities.

"I spent most of my time talking to God, more than to people. He was my partner, my friend, my teacher, my King, my sovereign, and I was so crazily religious that nothing else mattered."

Elie Wiesel, 1996

nose in his books, studying languages and religion. He was not one for outdoor games and sports, preferring to pray and contemplate spiritual issues.

As a child in a religious Jewish family, Elie devoted most of his young life to studying the Torah, the Talmud, and the mystical writings of the Kabbalah. Inspired by his grandfather, a deeply religious Hasidic Jew and a rabbi, little Elie started attending Yeshiva, or Jewish school, when he was just three years old.

While his parents approved of their son's intensely religious pursuits, they wanted to make sure he maintained a balanced perspective on life. They insisted he study more worldly, secular or non-religious subjects, along with modern Hebrew, so he could explore contemporary schools of philosophical thought.

"My life was a religious life," said Elie. "I studied...in elementary school and then high school, but always within the religious texts. My whole youth, really, was devoted to study."

Later in life, Elie remembered his father saying: "Whatever you want to study is all right with me, and I'll help you. But you must give me one hour a day for modern study." Together, Elie and his dad studied subjects such as psychology, astronomy, and music.

At home, the family spoke mostly Yiddish, but given Sighet's geographical location, the Wiesels could also speak Hungarian, Romanian, and German.

> *"My mother's dream was to make me into a doctor of philosophy; I should be both a PhD and a rabbi."*
>
> Elie Wiesel, in *Night*

Becoming Involved

Shlomo was a dedicated community leader who showed great concern for others. When Germany invaded Poland in 1939, Shlomo helped Jews escape to Hungary. This drive "to be involved" was a trait he passed on to Elie.

For Jews, every Saturday is the Sabbath, a day of rest. On this day, Shlomo visited inmates at the local prison, Elie's sisters attended to hospital patients, and Elie visited the mentally ill at the local psychiatric institution. With all his education, insight, and community involvement, young Elie was indeed a well-rounded boy.

It is surprising, then, that he and his family were so unaware of the dangers facing them— as Jews—as Adolf Hitler's German forces pushed farther and farther into Eastern Europe, rounding up and killing thousands of Jews as they went. Perhaps it was because Sighet was so geographically cut off that they thought they would be left alone. Perhaps it was because, in 1940, Sighet became part of Hungary, and Hungarian Jews were at first protected from Nazi persecution. Perhaps, wrote Elie in his book *Night,* it was because

The synagogue in Elie Wiesel's hometown of Sighet, Romania. A place for prayer and religious study, the synagogue was a center of young Elie's life as a Jew.

WHO WAS ADOLF HITLER?

Adolf Hitler was born in Austria, in a town near the German border, in 1899. By the 1930s, he had become a leader whose beliefs, words, and actions were such that even today many consider him to represent evil in its purest form.

After he fought in World War I, Hitler joined the National Socialist German Workers Party, or the Nazi Party, for short. He worked his way up through the ranks until he became party leader.

During his rise to power, he spent time in prison for trying to overthrow the ruling party of Germany. Still, by 1933, the Nazis had enough influence that Hitler became Chancellor, or head of the German government. Following his rise to power, Hitler made it illegal for any political party, other than the Nazi Party, to exist; and so, the "Nazification" of Germany began.

Hitler and his party controlled the content of the media, films, art, and books. They broke up trade unions and youth groups, replacing them with single, Hitler-approved organizations. They prohibited churches from preaching anything but Nazi beliefs.

Hitler also had the final say in Germany's legal matters, so nobody who opposed him ever received a fair trial. In 1935, laws were passed stripping all Jews of their rights as German citizens and banning them from public transportation and from such public places as theaters, restaurants, and parks.

By the late 1930s, Hitler had begun to ignore international agreements set in place after World War I. He took over Austria in 1938. A year later, when he invaded Poland, World War II began.

Hitler's attempt to control Europe and rid the world of minority groups he considered "inferior" continued for the next five years. Under his orders, millions of Jews were persecuted and killed. By the spring of 1945, it became clear that the Allied nations were about to defeat Hitler, Nazi Germany, and other Axis nations allied with him. When Hitler realized he was going to lose the war, he married his longtime companion, Eva Braun. The next day, he made his will and then shot himself. Eva Braun also killed herself by biting into a cyanide capsule. Days later, Germany surrendered, and World War II ended in Europe.

Adolf Hitler in 1937.

"London radio, which we listened to every evening, announced encouraging news" that a German defeat was close at hand.

Whatever the reason, the people of Sighet believed they were safe from the Nazi destruction. They even ignored the warnings of one of their townspeople, an awkward member of the Jewish community called Moishe the Beadle, a poor man who had helped Elie study the teachings of the Kabbalah.

The Beginning of the End

In 1942, when Nazis rounded up all foreign Jews in Hungary, Moishe was the only person taken from Sighet. Along with thousands of other non-Hungarian Jews removed from other towns, Moishe was sent to Poland to be executed, but he escaped by playing dead. He returned to Sighet to warn his friends and neighbors about the oncoming devastation. None of them believed his wild story. They thought he had gone mad.

Two years later, when uniformed Germans moved into Sighet, the people still did not suspect the horrors to come. Elie later wrote in *Night*:

"The officers were billeted [lodged] in private homes, even in Jewish homes. Their attitude toward their hosts was distant but polite. They never demanded the impossible, they made no offensive remarks, and sometimes even smiled at the lady of the house."

In March 1944, everything changed, and changed quickly. Hungarian police officers, who

DRAWING LINES ON THE MAP

Hitler and his Nazi Party took political power in Germany in 1933. For more than ten years, they were frighteningly successful in their quest to dominate Europe. Little by little, the German army invaded neighboring European nations, moving international borders as it went.

In 1938, Germany's borders expanded to the south and southeast, as Hitler invaded and took over Austria and parts of Czechoslovakia. In 1939, part of Poland became part of Germany. This move marked the beginning of World War II, as France and Britain supported Poland by declaring war on Germany.

Over the next five years, Germany pushed its way into neighboring nations in all directions. In 1940, because of a wartime agreement between Germany and the Hungarian government, the Hungarian border was also moved. It now included the part of Romania where Elie Wiesel and his family lived.

By 1943, most of Europe, as we know it today, was under German control, and what had been Austria, Czechoslovakia, and parts of Poland, Ukraine, and Lithuania were now part of Germany.

In 1945, the Allies, which by then included Canada, the United States, and the Soviet Union, beat Hitler's forces back. Eventually, Germany surrendered. Following its defeat, the country was divided between the Soviet Union (in the east) and France, Britain, and the United States (in the west)—into East Germany and West Germany. The two Germanys, together, were slightly smaller than pre-Nazi Germany.

This map shows the extent of Germany's control over most of Europe by 1943. With the exception of the Soviet Union to the east and, to the west, the United Kingdom, all of the dark- and light-gray areas shown here were occupied by Germany, had joined Germany as one of the Axis nations, or were incorporated into the new empire of "Greater" Germany. The countries in white were officially neutral during the war.

Iceland
(Britain)

Faroe Islands
(Britain)

Sweden

Finland

Soviet
(USSR)

Norway

Denmark

Ireland

United
Kingdom

Nether-
lands

General Government

German Empire

Belgium

Bohemia/
Moravia

Slovakia

Northern France

Hungary

Liechtenstein

Switzerland

Romania

Vichy France

Croatia

Monaco

Serbia

Bulgaria

Montenegro

Italy

Portugal

Spain

Albania
(Italy)

Vatican
City

Greece
(Italy)

German soldiers and Hungarian police round up Jews in Budapest, Hungary, in 1944. Hungary was allied with Germany in World War II, and when German troops occupied Hungary toward the end of the war, over 400,000 Jews in Hungary were deported. Most of them were sent to their deaths in the Auschwitz concentration camp.

had once been friends of the Jews and other citizens, united with the Nazis. Jewish leaders were arrested. Nazi soldiers and Hungarian police suddenly enforced curfews, closed Jewish shops, and stripped all Jews of their gold, jewelry, and everything else of value. The Jews of Sighet were no longer allowed to attend synagogue services. They were forced to wear yellow stars on their clothing.

In April, Hungarian police strung barbed wire around certain parts of the town, forming two ghettos and forcing all Jews to live within these prison-like enclosures. Fortunately for the Wiesels, their house was located within the larger of these ghettos, so they didn't have to move—but they took in relatives who had been driven from their homes.

THE YELLOW STAR: BADGE OF SHAME, BADGE OF HONOR

For centuries, the six-pointed Star of David, named after King David, the biblical Jewish leader, has been a symbol of Judaism and the Jewish people. Long before becoming as commonly known worldwide as it is today, the star was used in many parts of the Middle East, North Africa, and Europe, often by Jews themselves and frequently as a means of forcing Jews to identify themselves in non-Jewish cultures.

During World War II, all Jews in Nazi-occupied territory were forced to sew onto their clothing a yellow badge resembling the Star of David. In this context, the star was a public symbol designed to identify, humiliate, and segregate, or set apart, the men, women, and children who wore it. Any Jew who did not display the badge could be severely punished—even killed.

The yellow-star rule was, at first, only for Polish Jews. Then, in September 1941, Nazi leaders required that it be worn by all Jews in German-occupied territory—anyone over the age of six. Even shops owned by Jews were required to display a yellow star.

Since the Holocaust, the Star of David has become a symbol not just of Jewish identity but of the unity of the Jewish people. It is displayed in various forms of ornamentation, including jewelry, and a blue Star of David is part of the flag of the modern state of Israel.

The flag of modern-day Israel features the Star of David.

A collection of Stars of David from various concentration camps on display at the Beth Shalom Holocaust Memorial Centre, in the United Kingdom.

As shocking as this may seem to us today, the Jews of Sighet simply adjusted to their new way of life behind the barbed wire. As Elie would later write in *Night*: "Little by little, life returned to 'normal.' The barbed wire that encircled us like a wall did not fill us with real fear. In fact, we felt this was not a bad thing."

To the Jews of Sighet, the police and the Nazis had created a secure Jewish territory— "a small Jewish republic"—that protected them from the hostility and "hate-filled stares" of those outside the wire. For a few weeks, they lived in the ghettos without fear.

Then the Gestapo— the brutal German secret police—arrived in town. Elie and his family finally began to understand the reality of the threat facing them. Within days, the deportations, or forced departures, began.

"Most people thought that we would remain in the ghetto until the end of the war.... Afterward, everything would be as before. The ghetto was ruled by neither German nor Jew; it was ruled by delusion."

Elie Wiesel, in *Night*

Elie's family was assigned to the last group of Jews to leave Sighet. As the Wiesels waited their deportation orders, they watched procession after procession of friends and neighbors leaving their homes, each person carrying nothing but a small bundle of personal treasures. Men, women, and children, the sick and the elderly, trudged together to the railroad station, where they boarded waiting trains.

ANTI-SEMITISM: ANCIENT HATRED, MODERN FACE

Historically, the term "Semite" referred to people who were connected through languages called Semitic languages. These people included groups living in present-day Ethiopia, Yemen, Oman, Jordan, and Israel, among other places. Semitic languages include Hebrew, Arabic, and Aramaic. Today, however, the term "anti-Semitism" refers exclusively to prejudice or hatred against Jews.

Sadly, this hatred is not new to Jews. Some say it actually started in biblical times. We do know that about 2,000 years ago, in the Roman Empire, conflict erupted when Jews refused to worship Roman gods. Before long, Christianity became the official religion of the Roman Empire, and Rome became the seat of the Catholic Church. For centuries to come, Christians held to the Church's teaching that the Jews were collectively responsible for the killing of Jesus. By decree and due to various forms of persecution, Jews in many Christian countries were forced to flee to other parts of the world.

Since the Middle Ages, campaigns designed to get rid of Jews have occurred time and time again. Thousands of Jews have been killed during these times. Based mostly on religious hatred, anti-Semitism took on yet another facet in Europe of the 1800s—prejudice on ethnic or racial grounds. The view of Jews as being racially inferior to a mainstream race of white "Europeans" reached its peak in the most recent mass killing of Jews—that which took place during World War II, when Nazi Germany killed six million Jews in the Holocaust.

During a boycott of Jewish businesses in 1933, Nazi paramilitary stormtroopers force Jews to carry signs bearing such anti-Semitic slogans as "A good German doesn't buy from Jews."

Just when the Wiesels thought it was their turn to be herded out of town, they were given brief hope. When the soldiers rounded them up, they weren't ordered to the train station. Instead, they were directed to a home in the smaller ghetto, where they were to live while they awaited deportation. The guards forced everyone—even Elie's tiny sister Tzipora—to run to their new home. If they were too exhausted to run, they were beaten. For the first time in his life, Elie saw his father cry. When father, son, and family arrived at their new dwelling, the first thing they did was pray.

The Wiesels settled into their new home, using the furniture, dishes, and even food left by previous owners who'd had no time to prepare for their forced departure. At the same time, the Nazis and police were helping themselves to whatever was left behind in the homes in the larger, just-evacuated ghetto.

Despite all this upheaval, and despite the reality facing the Wiesels and the few other Jewish families still in Sighet, the people remained optimistic. They knew the tide was turning and the Germans were losing the war.

"We realized then that we were not staying in Hungary. . . . Our eyes were open. Too late."

They believed help would come before it was too late for those left in the ghetto.

Help did come for the Wiesels—in the form of their Christian housekeeper, Maria. The small ghetto was loosely guarded, so at this point, the family could still have escaped. Maria sneaked in and offered the Wiesels her cabin in the mountains as a hiding place. Elie's parents declined her offer, saying they preferred to keep the family with the Jewish community.

Four days later, in late May 1944, the family's time ran out. Early that morning, 15-year-old Elie, his father Shlomo, mother Sarah, elder sisters Hilda and Bea, and seven-year-old Tzipora were herded aboard a train bound for Auschwitz.

The Train to Hell

With 80 people crammed into each rail car, the heat was stifling. There was no room to sit down, no air, and no bathroom. The prisoners on the train had a bit of bread and a few pails of water to share for the journey. None of them knew how long they would be on the train or where they were headed.

They were locked in, their nerves were frayed, they were hungry and thirsty, and the stink in the cars became sickening. The worst moment for the captives came, however, when the train crossed the border from Hungary into Czechoslovakia. Until then, they had believed they were headed for a work camp somewhere within the Hungarian borders. Terror set in. "We realized then that we were not staying in Hungary," said Elie. "Our eyes opened. Too late."

Peering through the train car's windows, the prisoners saw rows of stark buildings, barbed wire, and flames shooting from a tall black chimney.

After four days on the rails, the train pulled into a station and stopped at Auschwitz. "When we arrived at Auschwitz, we didn't know what it meant, 'Auschwitz,' " Elie said. "Had we known, many of us would have gone into hiding [in Maria's cabin] in the mountains."

They had arrived at the Nazis' largest concentration camp, a massive complex in the south of modern-day Poland, where Jews were either forced into slave labor or killed. Peering through the train car's windows, the prisoners saw rows of stark buildings, barbed wire, and flames shooting from a tall black chimney.

A chilling "greeting" at an entrance to what was perhaps World War II's most infamous concentration camp, Auschwitz. The slogan Arbeit Macht Frei *(Work Makes One Free) served as a thin disguise for one of the camp's chief purposes during the war—to serve as a factory of death.*

Men with clubs shoved Elie and his family out of the cattle cars, forbidding them to bring with them their few cherished possessions. Soldiers pointed machine guns at them. German shepherds barked at them. An officer yelled, "Men to the left. Women to the right."

Elie veered left with his father, Shlomo. His mother, Sarah, and his three sisters, as instructed, moved to the right—not knowing they were on the path to the gas chambers. There was no chance to say goodbye. That was the last time Elie saw his mother—and it was in that moment that his sheltered childhood ended.

"I didn't know that this was the moment in time and the place where I was leaving my mother and Tzipora forever."

Elie Wiesel, in *Night*

MADWOMAN OR VISIONARY?

Throughout Elie's train trip to Auschwitz, a woman named Madame Schächter sobbed, moaned, and screamed. Over and over, she cried, "I see fire! I see flames, huge flames," wrote Elie in *Night*. When the others in the train car peered out into the darkness, they saw nothing. They convinced themselves she had gone mad, she was hysterical, or she was hallucinating. To quiet her and calm their own nerves, some beat her into silence. It didn't occur to any of them that she might have been having a vision of what was to come.

Were her episodes psychic glimpses into the near future—or insanity? In the face of events as horrific as those experienced during the Holocaust, how are humans to establish "usual" standards of sanity and insanity, reason and lunacy, or even good and evil? For decades, questions such as these have been among topics examined by book clubs, student study guides, and scholars discussing Elie Wiesel's *Night*.

A POINT OF INTEREST

Of the 15,000 Jews taken from Sighet, only 2,000 returned. Today, fewer Jews live in all of Romania than lived in pre-war Sighet.

Chapter 3
Auschwitz and Buchenwald

As 15-year-old Elie Wiesel watched his mother disappear, hand-in-hand with his little sister, he clung to his father's hand. Behind him, an elderly man was shot dead. In front of him were guards with clubs. All around him were noise and chaos. In the midst of this madness, Elie realized that the most important thing from this moment on, no matter what else happened, was that he and his father, Shlomo, stay together. As the horror of his new reality dawned on him, he knew neither he nor his dad could face Auschwitz alone.

Altered Reality

Elie and Shlomo lined up with the other men to be marched past the notorious Dr. Josef Mengele, the man who would decide their

A more experienced prisoner told father and son to lie about their ages.

fate—whether they would live or die. A more experienced prisoner told father and son to lie about their ages. Elie should say he was 18, rather than risk being considered a child too young to pull his weight, the man said. Similarly, Shlomo was to give his age as 40, rather than risk being considered too old to work at 50, his true age.

"Dr. Mengele was holding a conductor's baton, and he was surrounded by officers," wrote Elie in *Night*. "The baton was moving constantly, sometimes to the right, sometimes to the left.

"In no time, I stood before him.

" 'Your age?' he asked ...

" 'I'm eighteen.' "

A group of Hungarian Jewish mothers, children, elderly, and some who are sick or disabled await their fate— death in the gas chambers of Auschwitz. During a "selection" shortly after their arrival, they were set apart from others who were considered better able to work as slave laborers.

THE ANGEL OF DEATH

One of the first people Elie Wiesel encountered at Auschwitz—and one of the most villainous—was a small, well-groomed monster of a man named Dr. Josef Mengele, also known as the Angel of Death. He was one of the officers who decided which prisoners would live, and which would die. Over the years, Mengele also conducted horrific medical experiments on the inmates of Auschwitz, with a particular fascination for young twins. Countless pairs of children endured torturous surgeries, poisonings, and injections at his hands. Most of the children died.

Considered one of the Nazis' most vicious war criminals, Mengele escaped Germany after the war and was never captured. His path has since been traced to South America, where he died in 1979.

The "Angel of Death," Josef Mengele, at far left, is shown in his SS uniform with other Nazi officials at a resort in Germany especially constructed for Auschwitz military personnel and staff.

Instead of admitting he was a student, Elie told Mengele he was a healthy farmer, and with that, the baton pointed to the left—to life. Shlomo was also directed to the left. Father and son were still together. But that was the only positive thing about their new reality.

As they marched to the barracks that were to be their new home, the Wiesels saw flames rising from a ditch. They saw officers throwing babies into the fire. Then another fiery pit, this

A group of children liberated from Auschwitz by the Soviet Red Army in January 1945. Among these children were twins who were kept alive to be used in experiments by Josef Mengele.

one for adult bodies. They finally understood, in horror, that Auschwitz was a death camp. "How was it possible that men, women, and children were being burned and that the world kept silent?" Elie wondered. "All this could not be real. A nightmare perhaps...."

But it was real. Prisoners were being gassed, shot, or beaten to death. They were stripped of their clothing, and their remains were shoveled into pits of fire or into crematories, which were ovens where the bodies were burned to ash.

When Elie realized this could be his fate, he told his father he would rather kill himself by running into the electrified barbed wire. His father wept, so Elie stayed by his side. Another man said the Kaddish, the Jewish prayer for the dead. While some of the men prayed to God, Elie raged against the Creator he had always loved and worshiped. "Why should I

"Never shall I forget that smoke. Never shall I forget the small faces of the children whose bodies I saw trans-formed into smoke under a silent sky. Never shall I forget those flames that consumed my faith forever. ... Never shall I forget those moments that murdered my God and my soul and turned my dreams to ashes."

Elie Wiesel, in *Night*

sanctify [bless] His name?" he wrote years later. "The Almighty, the eternal and terrible Master of the Universe, chose to be silent. What were we to thank Him for?"

For the first time in his life, Elie began to question the God he had loved and trusted throughout his childhood, marking the start of an internal philosophical struggle that continues to this day.

Once inside the barracks, the men were forced to strip. SS officers checked out all the naked forms, seeking the strongest to assign the duty of shoveling bodies into the fires. Elie and Shlomo were not chosen for that task, but they had their heads shaved, were dunked in disinfectant, and were forced to run outside, naked in the cold, to a storeroom where SS men threw ill-fitting pants and shirts at them.

"All that was left was a shape that resembled me," wrote Elie of that moment in time. "My soul had been invaded—and devoured—by a black flame."

He had one last insult to endure that first day at Auschwitz. A man with a needle tattooed a serial number on the teenager's left forearm. No longer was he Elie Wiesel. He was now A-7713.

The boring routine ended soon enough, though.

NEW IDENTITY

Auschwitz was the only Nazi prison camp where prisoners were identified by serial numbers tattooed on their arms.

At first, numbers were sewn onto inmates' clothing, but that system didn't work for those prisoners who were stripped and killed. Once their clothing had been removed, there was no way to identify them. So the SS came up with the practice of tattooing the left forearm of each person who was not immediately executed upon arrival at the camp.

Ultimately, the SS assigned more than 400,000 serial numbers at Auschwitz. Elie Wiesel was A-7713.

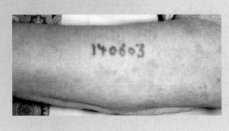

The tattooed forearm of a survivor of Auschwitz.

Brutal New World

For the next three weeks, thanks to a kind guard-in-charge, Elie and Shlomo settled into a dull routine. Their day consisted of coffee and bread in the mornings, soup at midday, and roll call at 6:00 P.M. They had nothing much else to do. By this time, only about 100 prisoners remained together in this particular barracks.

Men with trades or special skills had already been sent off and put to work.

But the boring routine ended soon enough. One day, Elie and his father were forced to walk for four hours with the other inmates. They ended up at Buna, the largest of Auschwitz's work camps. There, the inmates were assigned to various Kommandos, or work groups. Elie and Shlomo, again, managed to stay together. They were assigned to work with a group of orchestra musicians, who played a tune as the prisoners marched off to their workplaces each day.

The Wiesels did not play instruments, but after the daily musical march, they joined the orchestra Kommando as warehouse laborers. One of the musicians, a Polish violinist named Juliek, explained to Elie: "The work is neither difficult nor dangerous. Only Idek, the Kapo— a prisoner assigned to lead the work unit— occasionally has fits of madness, and then you'd better stay out of his way."

Elie discovered that Juliek was right on both counts. The work was simple and quiet. It involved such tasks as counting bolts, bulbs, and small electrical items, or loading parts into trucks. Juliek had also been right about Idek.

One day, when Idek was in a particularly bad frame of mind, he happened upon Elie and attacked "like a wild beast." He punched, beat, and crushed Elie's head and chest

The armband of an Oberkapo *(chief Kapo) at a Nazi concentration camp.*

"You are in Auschwitz. And Auschwitz is not a convalescent home. It is a concentration camp. Here, you must work. If you don't, you will go straight to the chimney. To the crematorium."

SS Guard

THE SS: BRUTAL ENFORCERS OF NAZI HATRED

The *Schutzstaffel*—"protection squadron"—better known as the SS—was founded in 1925 as a personal bodyguard service for Adolf Hitler. When Hitler became leader of Germany in 1933, it expanded into a harsh force of 50,000 members. By the time World War II started in 1939, the SS had grown to five times that number.

Among the better-known SS units were the Gestapo, or secret state police, and the brutal guards in charge of the concentration camps. SS officers were schooled in racial hatred and trained to turn a blind eye to human suffering. They carried out the campaign to exterminate Europe's Jews and other minorities. They also had to prove the racial "purity" of their own lineage back more than 200 years.

Left: the official insignia worn on most SS uniforms. Right: a military hat displaying two traditional emblems adopted by the Nazis—the swastika, with its crosslike arms bent at right angles, and the Totenkopf—*"death's head"—which came to be associated with the SS in particular. After the war, both the SS and the Nazi Party were outlawed as criminal organizations in Germany.*

until the teenager was covered with blood. On a different occasion, Idek gave Elie 25 lashes with a whip after Elie accidentally caught the Kapo in an inappropriate situation with a girl. Another time, Idek thought Shlomo wasn't working hard enough, and he beat the older man with an iron bar.

Later in life, Elie despaired that he had not gone to his father's aid the day of that beating. He recognized how dehumanized he had already become at Auschwitz:

"I had watched it all happening without moving. I kept silent. In fact, I thought of stealing away in order not to suffer the blows. What's more, if I felt anger at that moment, it was not directed at the Kapo but at my father. Why couldn't he have avoided Idek's wrath? That was what life in a concentration camp had made of me...."

The warehouse foreman, Franek, another Polish musician, befriended Elie and his father. Then he discovered Elie had a valuable gold

Prisoners were ordered back to their barracks, and SS men took cover. U.S. planes were coming!

crown on his tooth, and he wanted it. Elie refused to have his tooth pulled, so Franek launched a vicious campaign against Shlomo—slapping, tormenting, and beating him—until Elie relented. A friend of Franek pulled the gold crown with a rusty spoon.

Attack!

By early summer of 1944, the Allies were closing in on German-held territories. One morning, at Buna, a siren started screaming. Prisoners were ordered back to their barracks, and SS men took cover. U.S. planes were coming!

During the chaos of such attacks, it was relatively easy for prisoners to escape, so guards had instructions to shoot to kill those found outside their cellblocks. During this particular alert, the cooks had left two pots of hot soup outside when they ran for cover. For starving inmates, the sight of unattended soup was almost too much to bear. Most managed to fight the impulse to run and fill their stomachs, however, because "fear was greater than hunger." Except for one man.

As hundreds of prisoners watched with a mixture of envy and dread, the man crawled on his belly to the soup cauldrons. He slowly hoisted himself up over the edge and dove in for a mouthful of soup. A shot rang out. The man died just as the U.S. bombers began an hour-long assault on the Buna work factory.

Nobody was hurt in the attack—except for the man who had dared try to eat. Later that day, prisoners were forced to dispose of an unexploded bomb and to clean up the rubble of buildings that had been demolished in the raid.

A week later, the SS hanged a man accused of stealing during the air raid. After he died, the rest of the prisoners were made to parade past the hanging man, and forced to look him in the face.

Elie witnessed many hangings during his time at Buna. One of them was particularly horrific. A youth, accused of some offense, was to hang beside two older men. When the moment came, the men died instantly, but the boy, being too light to cause enough pressure on his neck, hung for half an hour before he stopped breathing. As he dangled there, the prisoners were forced to pass him, look at him "full in the face," and watch him die.

An elderly Jewish woman and several children are forced to make their way to the gas chambers of Auschwitz-Birkenau in 1944. During a "selection" shortly after their arrival, they were set apart from others who were considered better able to work as slave laborers.

A PORTRAIT OF AUSCHWITZ

Located in Oswiecim, Poland (a town called Auschwitz by the Germans), this largest of all Nazi concentration camps opened in May 1940. At first, it was used to house Polish resisters to Nazi rule. Within a year, the prisoner population had reached almost 11,000. It was here that the SS first experimented with gas chambers, killing 850 people in September 1941.

Before long, to relieve overcrowding at Auschwitz, the Nazis ordered construction of a second, larger facility—Auschwitz II, or Birkenau. Nearby German peasants were evicted from their homes to make room for what was to be the largest section of the camp. When it was complete, in early 1942, Birkenau, located nearly two miles (three kilometers) from the original barracks, had the capacity for almost 100,000 inmates. Within two years, it also housed four crematories, or "death factories," where hundreds of thousands of prisoners would be gassed to death and their bodies immediately burned.

In the area surrounding Auschwitz I, a number of sub-camps were constructed, the largest of which was Buna, established in October 1942. Inmates who lived here—including Elie and Shlomo Wiesel—were loaned out as slave labor to nearby mining operations, industrial plants, and chemical manufacturers. Buna held about 12,000 prisoners.

The entry point, by rail, leading to the infamous "death gate" at Auschwitz-Birkenau.

The Passing Seasons

Elie questioned his faith in God because of incidents such as the young boy who was brutally hanged. In the autumn, during Rosh Hashanah, the start of the new year on the Jewish calendar, while others praised God, Elie cursed him:

"Why would I bless Him? Because He caused thousands of children to burn in His mass graves? Because He kept six crematoria working day and night, including Sabbath and the Holy Days? Because in His great might, He had created Auschwitz, Birkenau, Buna, and so many other factories of death? How could I say to Him: Blessed be Thou?"

As 16-year-old Elie struggled to understand his Creator, Shlomo kept his faith strong. The two were separated for the first time— separated in their beliefs, and separated into different work units. Elie, still young and strong, had been transferred to the construction Kommando, where he hauled slabs of concrete 12 hours a day; Shlomo stayed at the warehouse.

Just before winter set in, the inmates went through another selection process. Dr. Mengele once again allowed Elie and his father to live, but Shlomo didn't pass with flying colors this time. His strength and energy were failing. Through the winter, the prisoners worked hard as their bodies suffered through the brutally cold weather. In January 1945, due to both an infection and the cold, Elie's foot began to swell. The camp doctor operated without anesthetic. "It will hurt a little, but it will pass," the doctor said.

Two days after Elie's surgery, the Allies neared Buna. The SS packed up the prisoners and marched them deeper into German territory. As a patient in the infirmary, Elie was to be left behind. He believed, though, that the SS would sooner kill the patients than allow them to be liberated by the coming Allies. In addition, he did not want to be separated from his father, so Elie joined the evacuation march—bleeding foot and all. After the war, he learned that the prisoners left behind in the infirmary had, in fact, been rescued within 48 hours.

Death March

During the 37-mile (60-km) trek to their new concentration camp, Gleiwitz, prisoners were forced to run, with armed SS guards by their sides. The SS shot anyone who could not keep up. All around Elie men died of cold, hunger, exhaustion, and gunshot wounds.

"I was thinking not about death, but about not wanting to be separated from my father. We had already suffered so much, endured so much together. This was not the moment to separate."

Elie Wiesel in *Night*

AUSCHWITZ TODAY

By the end of 1945, within months of the end of World War II, the Polish government had already begun working on plans to transform Auschwitz-Birkenau into a memorial museum. In 1946, before the memorial was fully open to the public, about 100,000 people visited the former camp. The visitors included many relatives of prisoners who had died there.

The Auschwitz-Birkenau Memorial and Museum officially opened on June 14, 1947. This date marked the seventh anniversary of the arrival of the first group of Polish prisoners at the camp. It stands as a memorial to the victims of the Holocaust. Visitors to the facility will see original buildings, barracks, guard towers, fences, crematories, gas chambers, and other structures. In addition, the museum has set up many exhibits to illustrate life—and death—at Auschwitz. Displays include photographs, prisoners' garments, SS artifacts, documents and maps, and a children's memorial area. The memorial also displays unsettling collections of stolen personal possessions, such as eyeglasses and new shoes, and hair shorn from prisoners when they arrived at the camp.

A Muslim student and a Jewish Holocaust survivor hold hands during a visit to Auschwitz-Birkenau in 2006. The two women are participants in a program called the March of Remembrance and Hope, which teaches students of different backgrounds about the dangers of prejudice. The program includes trips to Germany and Poland.

He considered giving up and letting himself die at the side of the road. "My father's presence was the only thing that stopped me," he wrote later. "He was running next to me, out of breath, out of strength, desperate. I had no right to let myself die. What would he do without me? I was his sole support."

At Gleiwitz, Elie was reunited with his musician friend, Juliek, who had managed to smuggle his violin with him on the march. The first night, as the men slept, Juliek played his violin.

Following the surrender of Nazi Germany in 1945, German civilians are forced to view the bodies of Jewish women who starved to death during a 300-mile (480-km) death march. Civilians had been directed by U.S. Army medics to dig up the bodies from the shallow grave into which the SS had dumped them. The bodies were later put into coffins and given a proper burial.

"He was playing a fragment of a Beethoven concerto," remembered Elie. "Never before had I heard such a beautiful sound. In such silence." By morning, Juliek was dead. After three days at Gleiwitz, and with the Allies close behind, the SS did another selection before moving the prisoners again. This time Shlomo was assigned to die, but Elie created such a fuss that, in the confusion, his father managed to slip, unnoticed, into the group selected to live.

All but 12 of the original 100 prisoners in Elie's railcar had perished.

Eating nothing but snow, the prisoners marched to a railroad track in the middle of nowhere. When a train finally came, the SS stuffed 100 men into each open-topped cattle car. Every so often, during the train's journey deeper into German territory, it would stop, so the prisoners and guards could toss out the dead bodies of men who had starved or frozen to death.

At one stop, a German worker walking by the train threw a piece of bread into a boxcar. "There was a stampede. Dozens of starving men fought desperately over a few crumbs," wrote Elie. Before long, other passersby started throwing bread, too, just to watch the spectacle of skeleton-like figures attacking each other. By the time the train arrived at its final destination, Buchenwald, a camp in the center of modern-day Germany, all but 12 of the original 100 prisoners in Elie's railcar had perished. They had traveled about 435 miles (700 km) from Auschwitz—and Shlomo was barely alive.

Saying Goodbye

As he did the day they arrived at Auschwitz, Elie held his father's hand as they entered

ANOTHER DEADLY STATISTIC

Of the 20,000 prisoners who left Buna, only 6,000 survived the journey to Buchenwald.

This photograph of crematories at Buchenwald was taken by U.S. soldiers in April 1945 after the camp's liberation by Allied forces. Still in the ovens are the bones of German women who were killed for opposing the Nazis.

Buchenwald. This time, though, it was so he could keep the older man from sitting down in the snow and dying. "Let me rest here at little," said Shlomo. "I beg of you. I'm so tired. No more strength." Elie refused to let go.

Almost immediately after their arrival, an air raid siren sent prisoners and guards into a frenzy, and Elie lost sight of his father. The next morning, after hours of searching, he found Shlomo, weak and burning with fever.

Over the next week, Shlomo began hallucinating, shivering, and suffering from dysentery, a painful intestinal ailment. He was so weak, he could no longer leave his bed to use the toilet. Whenever Elie left his side, to get bread or take a shower, Shlomo's fellow inmates beat him and stole his food to hurry the older man's death.

When Elie realized there was no hope for his father, he considered, for "a fraction of a second," taking Shlomo's ration of food and water for himself. The thought went in and out of his head so quickly, said Elie later, "but it left me feeling guilty."

During the night of January 28, 1945, as Shlomo called out to his son, crying in pain, hunger, and thirst, an SS officer clubbed him to death. By morning, Shlomo's body was already gone, and another man was in his bed. Elie has never forgiven himself for ignoring his father's cries that night.

> *"His last word had been my name. He had called out to me, and I had not answered. I did not weep, and it pained me that I could not weep. But I was out of tears."*
>
> Elie Wiesel in *Night*

The barracks at Buchenwald, where ill-fed, poorly clothed prisoners were crowded into narrow bunks. In this photo, Elie Wiesel (face circled) is shown with other Jewish slave laborers.

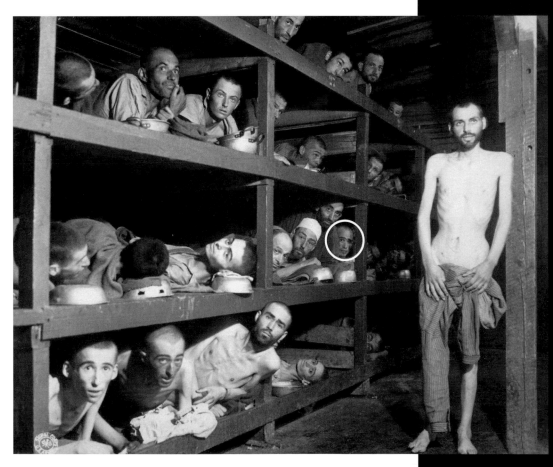

Chapter 4
Post-War Days and *Night*

After Elie Wiesel's father died in Buchenwald, the 16-year-old found himself alone in the world, without family for the first time in his life. After eight months of struggling to survive, side-by-side with his father, Elie had no will to continue the fight alone. "Nothing mattered anymore," he said. "After my father died, something in me died." He was transferred to a children's section of the camp, where 600 orphaned kids lived together—and, two months later, were rescued together.

Freedom

On April 6, 1945, with the Allies fast approaching, SS guards announced they would start "evacuating" prisoners, and they would no longer provide any food. For the next five days, the SS killed 10,000 Buchenwald prisoners a day—until the population was down to 20,000.

At that point, the guards decided to shoot the rest of the inmates all at once and demolish the camp before the Allies arrived. Thanks to an air-raid alert, however, they were forced to take cover. Their plan to slaughter the rest of the prisoners—including the children—was put on hold for a day.

U.S. soldiers examine items on display in the section of Buchenwald where children were kept. The words "PLACE FOR CHILDREN 5–15 years" were added.

The next morning, April 11, as the prisoners were herded together to be killed, a resistance movement rose up from within the camp and attacked the SS. "Armed men appeared from everywhere," wrote Elie in *Night*. "Bursts of gunshots. Grenades exploding. We, the children, remained flat on the floor of the block."

By noon, the SS had fled, the resistance had taken charge of the camp, and at 6:00 P.M., the first U.S. tanks rolled through the gates of Buchenwald. The liberators brought food, and the first thing Elie and the other prisoners did was eat. "That's all we thought about," he said. "No thoughts of revenge, or of parents. Only of bread."

Less than two weeks later, on May 7, 1945, Germany surrendered to the Allied Forces. World War II was over in Europe.

Life Begins Again

After liberation, and after eating too much of the wrong kinds of food for a person who had been on the verge of starving to death, Elie became very sick: "I was in a coma. I had blood poisoning." He wasn't the only one who fell ill at that time—5,000 of the 20,000 Buchenwald survivors died of intestinal ailments within weeks of their release from the camp. After ten days, Elie recovered but he was now an orphan.

A U.S. soldier poses beside a figure representing Adolf Hitler hanged by members of the Buchenwald inmate resistance. The inmates also wrote the graffiti on the barracks, which reads, in German, "Hitler must die for Germany to live."

PUSHING BACK

Secret, or underground, resistance organizations existed in every Nazi-occupied nation during World War II. Their members, usually known as partisans, risked their lives to help the Allies, ultimately playing a significant role in defeating the Nazis. In France alone, more than 100,000 people joined resistance movements.

Some partisans served as spies for the Allies, while others hid or otherwise protected persecuted people, including Jews. Resistance organizations forged documents, staged raids on Nazi offices to get information, and helped POWs (prisoners of war) escape.

In the case of Auschwitz, one member of the Polish resistance actually volunteered to be imprisoned at the camp, so he could send reports to the outside world about SS brutality. He eventually escaped, but nobody believed his horror stories, until two other inmates escaped and told the same stories.

The resistance group within Auschwitz created an underground, or secret, newspaper that somehow made it to Poland. One prisoner had managed to smuggle in a shortwave radio, so the resistance could also send messages from Auschwitz directly to Polish government officials in exile outside of Poland.

Many members of resistance organizations within Germany and in German-occupied territory were German citizens who opposed Nazi rule. They pretended to support Hitler, so they could be in positions to gather information for the Allies, get weapons to prisoners, and sabotage Nazi military operations.

Irena Sendler, a Catholic social worker who was part of the Polish underground, smuggled 2,500 Jewish children out of the Warsaw Ghetto, secured false identification papers for them, and found them safe homes outside the ghetto.

Dutch resistance members during a briefing with U.S. troops in Eindhoven, Netherlands.

French partisans in occupied Paris.

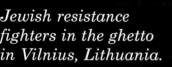

Jewish resistance fighters in the ghetto in Vilnius, Lithuania.

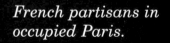

Soviet partisans operating behind German lines in Belarus

THE CAMPS: BUSINESSLIKE TERROR

While Auschwitz was the largest and among the most brutal of the World War II Nazi concentration camps, it certainly wasn't the only one. Today, the German government estimates the number of camps at about 1,200. Other sources, including the Jewish Virtual Library and the United States Holocaust Memorial Museum, suggest 15,000 to 20,000 camps existed during Adolf Hitler's reign (1933–1945).

Along with ghettos and patterns of persecution, assaults, and killings carried out by Germany, the concentration camps were part of a carefully planned program of terror. Most of the victims in the camps were civilians, but they also included POWs. Captured Soviet troops were especially singled out for cruel treatment. Some camps simply served as places to hold prisoners awaiting transportation to other facilities. Others were places of forced labor, and some—the most sinister—were extermination camps, designed for mass murder.

Toward the end of World War II, Jews were, by far, the people most often taken to, and killed at, Nazi concentration camps. The Nazis also targeted other groups the Nazis considered inferior "races." These included Poles and Romanies (Gypsies). Other people the Nazis felt would dilute the "purity" of the so-called Aryan race were also imprisoned. These included disabled adults and children, homosexuals, and Jehovah's Witnesses. Also targeted were political enemies and members of unions and other labor organizations.

A Soviet slave laborer identifies a former SS guard at Buchenwald who had brutally beaten prisoners. The prisoner, along with Elie Wiesel and other inmates, was liberated by U.S. forces in April 1945.

A Jewish organization called the Children's Rescue Society sent Elie, along with about 400 other orphaned children, from Germany to France to start new lives, and to study. For the next two years, Elie lived in several French homes and orphanages.

Before he left Germany, Elie had studied lists of survivors' names, hoping to find members of his family, but he found neither his mother nor his sisters. "That's why I went to France," he said in a 2006 interview. "Otherwise I would have gone back to my hometown of Sighet."

One day, some journalists came to the French orphanage where Elie was living at the time and took photos of him and another boy playing chess. Elie's older sister Hilda, who was also living in France, happened to see Elie's photo in the newspaper. She contacted the orphanage, and days later, brother and sister were together again. "Otherwise, it would have taken years for us to be reunited," said Elie. "Since then, I have had a very soft spot for journalists, so I became a journalist."

Within a year, Hilda and Elie were also reunited with their sister Bea, who had returned to Sighet after the war, hoping to find her siblings there. "Many months passed before Bea found out I was alive," wrote Elie in his memoirs, *All Rivers Run to the Sea*. "Someone told someone who saw her in Sighet." The trio met up in Antwerp, Belgium. To this day, the siblings have never discussed their Holocaust ordeals with each other. Bea died of cancer in 1974.

Like the other young Holocaust survivors who had moved to France, Elie had been offered the

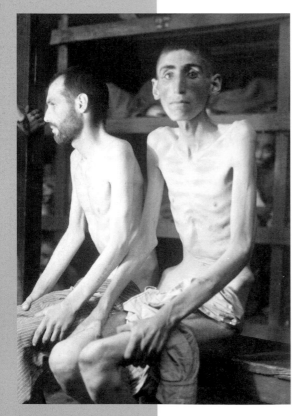

choice of taking religious or non-religious studies in his new homeland. Despite his continuing bitterness toward God, he chose to return to the religious studies he had pursued during his childhood in Romania. He also studied French with a tutor before

These slave laborers were on the verge of starvation at the time of their liberation from Buchenwald. They told U.S. troops that they weighed an average of 160 pounds (72.5 kg) each before their internment. At the time of their freedom, 11 months later, they averaged only 70 pounds (32 kg).

enrolling, in 1948, at the Sorbonne, a respected, historical university in Paris. There, he studied languages and literature, philosophy and psychology.

During his years in France, Elie also studied with a Jewish scholar named Shushani, who—like Moishe the Beadle back in Romania—encouraged Elie to question everything, including God.

After a year at the Sorbonne, where Elie's interest in journalism continued to grow, he started writing for a French newspaper called *L'Arche*. He supplemented his income by translating, teaching Hebrew, and working as a choirmaster. In 1949, Elie visited Israel for the first time, as a reporter for *L'Arche*. While there, he arranged a job for himself as a Paris correspondent for an Israeli newspaper called *Yedioth Ahronoth*.

For the next few years, Elie juggled his schoolwork with his budding journalism career, By 1952, the load became too much for him. He left the Sorbonne without completing his doctoral dissertation. This was a major graduate research project in which he was comparing different religious concepts. He started traveling the world—to Asia, North America, Israel, Africa, South America, and throughout Europe—working full time as a journalist.

In 1954, his career as a reporter took him to an interview that would change his life.

"My survival was arbitrary. I don't want to call it a miracle because it would mean that God performed a miracle for me alone. It means he could have performed more miracles for others who were worthier than I.... It was sheer luck."

Elie Wiesel, 2002

After World War II, Elie Wiesel learned French and studied in Paris at the Sorbonne, shown here. During this time, he became a journalist, writing for newspapers in France and Israel.

Night

In 1954, Elie wanted to interview the Prime Minister of France, Pierre Mendès-France, for an article he was writing. When his request for a meeting was declined, he refused to be put off. He came up with another plan to reach the French leader. He set up an interview with the Prime Minister's teacher and friend, François

Mauriac, a Nobel Prize winner who was also a famous French Catholic writer. Elie's goal was to convince Mauriac to introduce him to Mendès-France, so he could conduct his interview.

Mauriac agreed to meet with the young journalist, but when they met, Mauriac only wanted to talk about Jesus and His suffering. "He was in love with Jesus," said Elie. "He spoke only of Jesus. Whatever I would ask, [the answer was] Jesus."

In his frustration, Elie tried to bring the subject back to the Prime Minister. "When he said 'Jesus' again, I couldn't take it," said Elie. "I said, 'Mr. Mauriac, 10 years or so ago I saw children, hundreds of Jewish children, who suffered more than Jesus did on his cross, and we do not speak about it.' "

Embarrassed by his outburst, and emotional over the subject he had just raised, Elie picked up his things and ran out of the room, sobbing. Mauriac caught up with him, brought him back

French writer François Mauriac encouraged Elie Wiesel to write about his experiences during the Holocaust. Mauriac wrote the forward to the first French edition of Elie's memoir, Night, *published in 1958.*

into the privacy of the interview room, and sat with the young man as he wept. "And then," remembered Elie, "without saying anything [else], he simply said, 'You know, maybe you should talk about it.'"

After his liberation from Buchenwald, while he was still in the hospital in Germany, Elie had considered writing down his experiences in the concentration camps. Instead, he had made a promise to himself at that time that he would not tell his story for at least ten years. Later in life, he said:

> "I knew I was going to write to bear witness. I had to, because not to bear witness to an event that one lived is a betrayal of that event. But I didn't know how. I was afraid of not finding the words. And I come from a mystical background [through Kabbalah] where one can purify language through silence, and that's why I was waiting for 10 years."

When Elie met Mauriac, the ten years he had vowed to wait before writing about his experiences had almost passed, and Mauriac persuaded the young man to get started. Elie spent the next year writing a 900-page manuscript in Yiddish. A publisher in Buenos

GIVING A VOICE TO SILENCE

Elie Wiesel still has the original 900-page version of *Un Di Velt Hot Geshvign (And the World Kept Silent)*. "It's testimony," he said in a 1978 interview with *The Paris Review*. "Therefore, I believe it should be kept, and one day I might publish it, because I have no right not to. It's not mine."

CHILDREN OF THE HOLOCAUST: THE GIRL WHO KEPT THE DIARY

Anne Frank was born in Frankfurt, Germany, in 1929. When she was four, her parents, fearing Hitler's new regime, moved the family to safety in Amsterdam, the capital city of the Netherlands. Seven years later, the Nazis invaded the Netherlands, and the Franks were in danger once again. Jews were harassed; they were forced to wear yellow stars; their businesses were closed down; and they were not allowed out of their homes at certain times of day.

Anne's parents, Otto and Edith, knowing worse treatment was to come for the family, took their children into hiding—into a secret attic behind an office in a non-Jewish friend's business. Soon, four other Jews joined the Frank family in their tiny, hidden home.

For two years, the eight tenants lived quietly together, until August 4, 1944, when an anonymous caller— whose identity remains unknown to this day— betrayed them. The Gestapo arrested Anne and her family and sent them to Auschwitz.

Three months later, Anne and her sister Margot were transferred to another camp, Bergen-Belsen, where both died in March 1945, a few weeks before British troops liberated the camp. Anne's mother died in Auschwitz. Her father survived and was freed on January 27, 1945.

This postage stamp commemorating the life of Anne Frank was issued by the Netherlands in 1980. While her family was in hiding, Anne kept a diary that her father, Otto, typed out and had published in 1947. The Diary of a Young Girl *has become one of the best-known, best-selling books about the Holocaust. It also served as the inspiration for* The Diary of Anne Frank, *a dramatic interpretation of Anne's life that was made into a play, two movies, a TV serial, and an opera.*

CHILDREN OF THE HOLOCAUST: THE GIRL WITH THE SUITCASE

When Hana Brady, a Czechoslovakian Jew, was 13 years old, she and her brother George were sent to Auschwitz. Their parents had been taken away a year earlier and were never heard from again. Hana was killed upon her arrival.

More than 50 years later, Fumiko Ishioka, a curator planning an exhibition about children of the Holocaust for a museum in Tokyo, Japan, visited Auschwitz. She asked if she could borrow some items that had belonged to children at the camp. She hoped that, by viewing keepsakes of children their own age, kids in Japan would gain a deeper, more personal understanding of the Holocaust—an event that had taken place thousands of miles (km) and an eternity in time from their own lives. One of the objects she received for her exhibition turned out to be Hana Brady's suitcase. Fumiko knew that she had come across a treasure. Here were cherished items that represented everything poor Hana was allowed to keep with her in the shattered hope of returning to her life in Czechoslovakia.

Over the next few years, even after the exhibition closed, Fumiko continued to research Hana's life. She discovered that Hana's brother, George, had survived the war and was living in Toronto, Canada. She went to visit him, and while she was there, a radio reporter, Karen Levine, happened to hear the story of Hana, George, and Fumiko. Karen made a radio documentary about the brother and sister and the curator's detective work that had brought their stories—and through them, their lives—together again. In 2002, Karen wrote a children's book called *Hana's Suitcase*, which has since become the basis of a play and a movie.

Hana Brady, on whose life a book, a play, and a documentary movie have been based. In the movie, Inside Hana's Suitcase, *the actual suitcase was replaced by a replica after the original was destroyed in a warehouse fire set by a group of neo-Nazis in Birmingham, England.*

THE BOOK BEFORE *NIGHT*

In a book of his memoirs, *All Rivers Run to the Sea*, Elie talks about an editor who in 1956 expressed an interest in acquiring a work of fiction. Elie promptly set out to write a novel "in a week or two" under the pen name Elisha Carmeli. Elie calls the book, which the editor published as *Silent Heroes*, "a romantic spy novel" involving two Israeli intelligence agents, a man and a woman, who are "desperately in love." According to his memoir, Elie barely recalls many other details of the book, although he does remember that "all my characters die at the end, since I wasn't sure what else to do with them."

Aires, Argentina, edited the work down to 245 pages and published it in 1956 as *Un Di Velt Hot Geshvign (And the World Kept Silent)*. Elie dedicated the book to his parents and younger sister Tzipora, who had not survived the war.

That same year, Elie moved to New York City to become a full-time U.S. correspondent for the Israeli newspaper *Yedioth Ahronoth*. Shortly after he arrived, he was hit by a taxicab and was seriously injured. He spent months in the hospital and was confined to a wheelchair for about a year.

Elie was not able to return to France to renew his expired French identity card because he could not travel during that time. Without that, he was not allowed to apply for a U.S. visa. On the other hand, Elie found he was eligible to apply for U.S. citizenship. He submitted an application.

Meanwhile, as he recovered from his accident, Elie focused more time on his writing, spending about four hours a day working on book projects.

He condensed *And the World Kept Silent* and translated it into French, but it was two years before a publisher agreed to print it. "Mauriac was the most famous author in Europe, and he brought the book personally from publisher to publisher," said Elie. "They didn't want it. It was too morbid, they said." Mauriac eventually

CHILDREN OF THE HOLOCAUST: THE BOY ON TV

A French Jew born in Paris in 1926, Robert Clary survived a number of concentration camps, including Buchenwald. After his liberation at age 19, he returned to Paris and continued a singing career he had started before his capture. At 23, he moved to the United States, where he performed in nightclubs and on Broadway, before moving into film and television work. Ironically, Robert is best known for his portrayal of Corporal Louis LeBeau on the TV show *Hogan's Heroes*, a comedy about Allied prisoners in a German POW camp during World War II. The show ran for six seasons (1965–1971). In 1982, Robert was the subject of a serious documentary titled *Robert Clary A-5714, A Memoir of Liberation.*

Robert Clary (lower right, wearing beret) is shown with other cast members in a publicity shot for the popular CBS comedy Hogan's Heroes.

found a publisher willing to take a risk, and *La Nuit* was published in 1958.

When it came time to find a publisher for the English version, called *Night*, the author and his friend Mauriac met similar resistance. "It went from publisher to publisher," said Elie. "All of them refused it. They gave the same reasons, until a small publisher picked it up."

In 1960, after more than 15 other publishers had rejected the manuscript, Hill & Wang, a tiny, independent publishing house that had just started up a few years earlier, agreed to publish Elie Wiesel's *Night*.

That book, one of dozens Elie would write, marked the starting point on a journey that would lead him to worldwide honor, respect, and recognition.

"I wrote [Night] for the other survivors who found it difficult to speak. I wanted to tell them, 'Look, you must speak. As poorly as we can express our feelings, our memories, we must try.' ... I wrote it for them, because the survivors are a kind of endangered species."

Elie Wiesel, 1996

Chapter 5
"A Messenger to Mankind"

Elie Wiesel's book *Night* was not an instant success. It sold just 1,000 copies in its first year and a half on the market. Elie continued to write, however, penning two works of fiction within the next year. Both books, *Dawn* and *The Accident* (later re-titled *Day*) were based on Elie's real-life experiences as a concentration camp survivor. In 1962, Elie wrote *The Town Beyond the Wall*, a novel about an imaginary return trip to his hometown of Sighet, Romania. Two years later, the year the book was published, Elie made the trip to his childhood home for real.

Moving Forward, with a Look Back

Before Elie returned to the town where he was born, he decided that New York City would become his new hometown. Years earlier, while recovering from his car accident, Elie had applied for U.S. citizenship, and in 1963, it became official—he became a citizen of the United States. In a 2007 interview, Elie said:

"I never had a passport in my life. In France, I was stateless [a refugee]. Here in America finally I became a citizen. I can't tell you what I felt. I felt so proud. The highest honor I've

received at universities is nothing compared to
the fact that I have a passport."

With his new U.S. passport, Elie took the trip to Sighet, a town he had not seen since he had been loaded into a cattle car with his family and taken away to Auschwitz 20 years earlier. When he visited Sighet this time, he didn't recognize it:

"Not because it had changed so much, but quite
the opposite: because it had not changed.
Everything remained the same—the streets,
gardens, houses, schools, shops. Only the Jews
were no longer there. They had all been driven
out ... and yet the town seemed to get along
without them."

After his visit to Sighet, Elie narrated a documentary about the mass deportation of the town's Jews—and how little impact the event seemed to have on the non-Jewish population. The film, titled *Sighet, Sighet,* premiered in 1964.

That same year, Elie earned the Ingram Merrill Award. This was the first of dozens of writing honors he would receive during his lifetime—and he continued churning out book after book. He wrote two more works related to the suffering of Jews during and after the Holocaust (*The Gates of the Forest* and *Legends of Our Time*) before he moved on to other related subjects.

In 1966, after a visit to the Soviet Union, Elie wrote *The Jews of Silence* about the plight of Russian Jews. After the 1967 Arab-Israeli War,

THE WORD "HOLOCAUST"

Some people—including Elie Wiesel himself—credit Elie with coining the term "Holocaust" in reference to the mass killings carried out by the Nazis during World War II. It is a word of Greek origin that means "sacrifice by fire." Elie said when he first used it, it was because it fit in perfectly with the biblical essay he was writing. "The word had so many implications," he said, "that I felt it was good. Then it became accepted, and everybody used it."

A number of scholars and other researchers say crediting Elie with coining the phrase is an exaggeration. They say the word was, in fact, used in this context before that—but it wasn't until a TV miniseries, titled *Holocaust*, aired in 1978 that the word became commonly used in our culture.

he wrote *A Beggar in Jerusalem* (1968) about Jews in that region, a novel that earned the Prix Medici, one of France's top writing awards.

After a self-imposed ten-year silence following his liberation from Buchenwald, Elie found he

Elie Wiesel signs copies of his award-winning novel, A Beggar in Jerusalem, *in 1968, the year the book appeared in French. The English translation was published two years later, in 1970.*

had a lot to say. He continued writing at a rapid pace, penning 18 more literary works in the next 15 years. These included novels, semi-autobiographical works of fiction, collections of essays, and a play.

New Family, New Directions

During this time of frenzied writing, Elie met a new writing collaborator, Marion Erster Rose, a fellow concentration camp survivor. Born in Austria, this mother of one daughter was also a writer and editor. She and Elie married on April 2, 1969, in Jerusalem, and three years later, they celebrated the birth of their son, Shlomo Elisha, named after Elie's father. Marion has done the translating—or overseen the translation—of all the work Elie has written since they met.

Elie's books, and their increasingly global subject matter, began to earn the writer international attention. Elie recognized that he could use his growing fame to help humanitarian causes around the globe. He started speaking out about the situation of oppressed peoples around the world. These included Jews in the Soviet Union, blacks in South Africa, victims of genocide in the former Yugoslavia, Cambodian refugees, and people dying of famine in Africa, among other humanitarian causes. He found himself in demand as a speaker and guest lecturer around the world.

"My son changed me. Once you bring life into the world, you must protect it. We must protect it by changing the world."

Elie Wiesel

Elie is shown in this 1989 photo with his wife, Marion, and their son, Shlomo Elisha, then about 17 years old.

During this time, Elie also began teaching, first as a Distinguished Professor of Judaic Studies at City University of New York. He held this position for four years. Later, he became the first Henry Luce Visiting Scholar in Humanities and Social Thought at Yale University (1982–1983). From 1976 until 2011,

In 1984, Elie presided over the groundbreaking ceremony for the United States Holocaust Memorial Museum.

he served as a professor in the Departments of Humanities, Philosophy, and Religion at Boston University, where he taught a course titled "Literature of Memory."

He continues to present a public lecture series at Boston University. His books are widely used in the classes there, and his writing is the subject of a pair of courses at the university.

Awards and honors for Elie poured in from around the world. He received literary awards from France, Israel, the United States, and Belgium. Humanitarian, heritage, spiritual, and academic awards came from nations around the globe. Elie also was awarded national decorations, such as the U.S.

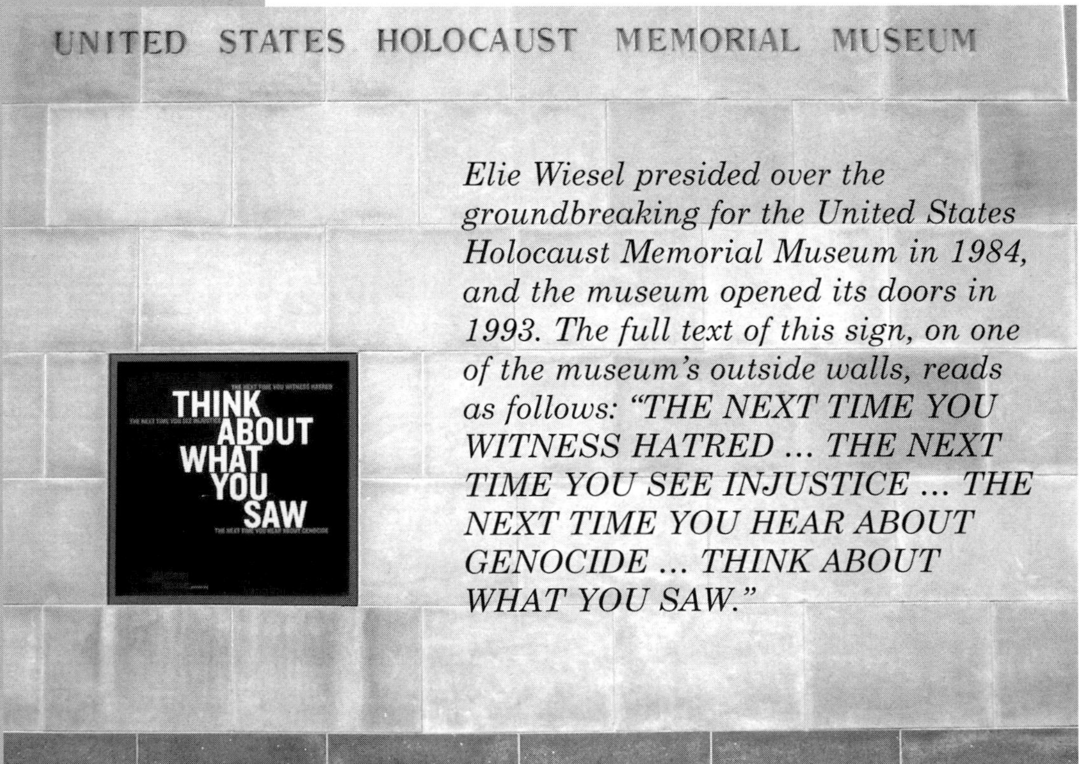

UNITED STATES HOLOCAUST MEMORIAL MUSEUM

THINK
ABOUT
WHAT
YOU
SAW

Elie Wiesel presided over the groundbreaking for the United States Holocaust Memorial Museum in 1984, and the museum opened its doors in 1993. The full text of this sign, on one of the museum's outside walls, reads as follows: "THE NEXT TIME YOU WITNESS HATRED ... THE NEXT TIME YOU SEE INJUSTICE ... THE NEXT TIME YOU HEAR ABOUT GENOCIDE ... THINK ABOUT WHAT YOU SAW."

GOD ON TRIAL

Since his first day at Auschwitz, Elie Wiesel has questioned the God he worshiped as a child. How could a loving Creator allow terrible things—such as the Holocaust—to happen? Some of Elie's books have dealt directly with this question. Others have featured characters who are facing their own spiritual dilemmas.

In 1978, Elie wrote a play called *The Trial of God*, inspired by a scene he witnessed at Auschwitz—three rabbis judging God for His role in the Holocaust. The play is set in a different, long-ago time, and it's written as a comedy. Elie tried writing the story first as a novel, then as a poem, then as a conversation between two characters. "It didn't work," he said. So he tried making it into a play. "Then I decided I would move the same theme back to the 16th century. And it worked. It's no longer in a [concentration] camp … and it's no longer a tragedy."

It is still a trial, however, with God as the defendant accused of "hostility, cruelty, and indifference." The play has been performed at a number of small venues in Europe and the United States. In 2008, the BBC (British Broadcasting Corporation) produced a television play, called *God On Trial*, based on the trial of God that Elie witnessed in Auschwitz.

Congressional Gold Medal of Achievement and admission into France's Legion of Honor. He was recognized internationally with awards, too, such as the International Holocaust Remembrance Award, the Humanitarian Award from the International League for Human Rights, and the Freedom Award from the International Rescue Committee.

DAYS OF REMEMBRANCE

Every year since 1981, the U.S. Congress has named eight days in late April or early May as Days of Remembrance of the Victims of the Holocaust. It is a time to remember Holocaust victims and participate in related educational programs.

A National Civic Commemoration is held at the U.S. Capitol in Washington, D.C., with other events around the country, and at U.S. military stations around the world. In 2005, the United Nations declared January 27 as International Holocaust Remembrance Day, to commemorate the date in 1945 when Soviet troops liberated the largest Nazi concentration camp, Auschwitz-Birkenau.

While many countries around the world hold commemorative events on January 27, some nations have set aside different days to remember the wartime atrocities. In France, a commemoration is held on July 16, the anniversary of the day in 1942 that more than 13,000 Jews were arrested in Paris and deported to Auschwitz. In Romania, the National Day of Commemorating the Holocaust is October 9, the anniversary of the first deportation in 1942 of Romanian Jews. In Poland, Holocaust Remembrance Day, April 19, marks the anniversary of the beginning of the most significant Jewish revolution against the Nazis—the uprising in the Warsaw Ghetto in 1943.

Far left: Two women wearing yellow stars in German-occupied Paris are shown in 1942, prior to their being rounded up and sent to Auschwitz. Right: Two members of the Jewish resistance are shown following the suppression of the Warsaw Ghetto Uprising in 1943. Each of these events—the deporting of French Jews to Auschwitz and the Warsaw Ghetto Uprising—is commemorated in France and Poland, respectively, as the focus for each nation's Holocaust remembrance day.

In 1978, U.S. President Jimmy Carter appointed Elie as the Chairman of the President's Commission on the Holocaust (later renamed the U.S. Holocaust Memorial Council), a position he held for eight years. Under Elie's leadership, the organization recommended the creation of annual Days of Remembrance, an eight-day event that takes place in the United States in late April or early May. It also recommended creating a museum dedicated to remembering the Holocaust.

In 1984, Elie presided over the groundbreaking ceremony for the United States Holocaust Memorial Museum in Washington, D.C. The museum opened nine years later.

Perhaps Elie Wiesel's greatest honor—and his greatest international acknowledgement—came in 1986, when he was presented with the Nobel Peace Prize, an annual award that recognizes an individual's, or organization's, humanitarian work in such areas as human rights, international mediation, and arms control.

This replica of a boxcar used to transport Jews and other victims of the Holocaust to death camps is one of the exhibits at the United States Holocaust Memorial Museum in Washington, D.C.

A WORD WITH THE PRESIDENT

In April 1985, U.S. President Ronald Reagan presented Elie Wiesel with the Congressional Gold Medal, one of the highest honors the government can bestow on a civilian. At the ceremony, Elie startled the audience with his acceptance speech.

He begged the President to cancel an upcoming visit to a German military cemetery, where Reagan intended to pay tribute to German World War II veterans buried there—including some SS soldiers. "May I, Mr. President, implore you to do something else," said Elie. "That place is not your place. Your place is with the victims of the SS."

Millions of people heard Elie's words—many for the first time—because the ceremony was televised nationally. Later, Elie said he considered this moment to be the "real breakthrough" in raising awareness of his book *Night* and of his humanitarian messages.

In the end, the President did not cancel his cemetery visit, but he quickly added a stop at a former concentration camp named Bergen-Belsen to his schedule. Jewish protestors, joined by World War II veterans and politicians, greeted him there.

Elie Wiesel receives the Congressional Gold Medal from President Ronald Reagan at the White House in April 1985.

THE NOBEL PRIZE:
DISTINGUISHED COMPANY

Every year, in addition to the Nobel Peace Prize, Nobel Prizes are awarded to people who have made distinguished contributions in four other fields—physics, chemistry, physiology or medicine, and literature. Since 1901, achievements in all these categories have been honored with the prize named for Alfred Nobel, a wealthy Swedish poet, playwright, scientist, and inventor of dynamite. When he died in 1896, Nobel left money in his will to establish the annual awards, which are presented every December in Stockholm, Sweden (prizes in physics, chemistry, medicine, and literature), and in Oslo, Norway (peace). Each Nobel Prize winner gets a medal, diploma, and money.

HOLOCAUST DENIERS

Despite masses of historical evidence, including detailed records and photos produced by the Nazis themselves, there are people who say the Holocaust never happened—or at least, if it did, it wasn't all that "bad." Some of those who deny the existence of the Holocaust spread their false messages on websites, while others deliberately "crash" websites created by Jewish organizations, Holocaust museums, and legitimate discussion groups. Others

place ads in student newspapers, hoping to convince young people that the Holocaust is a hoax.

Canada and nations in Western Europe have hate crime and racial discrimination laws. Some Holocaust deniers have been tried and convicted under these laws. In the United States, the First Amendment guarantees the right of free speech, no matter what the message. It does not, however, mean that media outlets are obligated to print Holocaust-denier information.

For decades, British writer David Irving has been known for his words and actions promoting the denial of the Holocaust. His activities have gotten him arrested, deported, and banned from Canada, Germany, Austria, and Italy. In other nations, including France, the United States, and the United Kingdom, protests and legal challenges have occurred against him and his writings. In this photo, he is shown at the time of his deportation from Canada in 1992.

"Elie Wiesel is a messenger to mankind. His message is one of peace, atonement [righting or accepting responsibility for a wrong], and human dignity," wrote the Nobel Committee when it announced that Elie was to receive the award. "[His] commitment, which originated in the sufferings of the Jewish people, has been widened to embrace all repressed peoples and races."

On December 10, 1986, in the presence of the King of Norway, Elie accepted the Nobel Peace Prize in Oslo. At his side were his wife, Marion, 14-year-old son, Shlomo Elisha, and sister Hilda. Along with the medal, certificate, and prestige of the Nobel Prize came a cash award of almost $290,000, money that would soon help Elie advance his mission to help others.

> "We must always take sides. Neutrality helps the oppressor, never the victim. Silence encourages the tormentor, never the tormented. Sometimes we must interfere. When human lives are endangered, when human dignity is in jeopardy, national borders and sensitivities become irrelevant. Wherever men or women are persecuted because of their race, religion, or political views, that place must—at that moment— become the center of the universe."
>
> Elie Wiesel, Nobel Prize Acceptance Speech, 1986

Chapter 6
Into the 21st Century

Within months of winning the 1986 Nobel Peace Prize, and using some of the cash award that came with it, Elie Wiesel and his wife Marion established the Elie Wiesel Foundation for Humanity, an organization dedicated to fighting indifference, prejudice, and injustice. Over the next six years, the foundation staged six international conferences. These events brought together Nobel Prize winners from around the world to share ideas and brainstorm solutions for humanitarian crises. At the same time, Elie continued to write and to lend his voice to campaigns against genocide and oppression around the world. He never wavered in his mission to make sure the Holocaust would never be forgotten.

"A museum is a place, I believe, that should bring people together, a place that should not set people apart."

Building a Legacy

A year after he won the Nobel Peace Prize, Elie was forced to relive some of his concentration camp experiences when he was called to testify against one of the cruelest of all war criminals, Klaus Barbie. Barbie was known as "The Butcher of Lyon" for his particularly monstrous treatment of Jews and French resistance fighters in Lyon, France, during World War II. In 1987, he was tried and sentenced to life in prison. He died of leukemia four years later, at age 77.

While Elie had never suffered personally at the hands of Barbie, a Jewish group in Lyon asked him to testify, in general, about the Nazis' wartime atrocities. On June 3, 1987, the New York Times reported that Elie testified about his "personal memories of Auschwitz, of the silence of millions of victims, and of what he called the unique nature of the Nazi campaign to wipe out the Jews":

The official photograph of Klaus Barbie, the infamous "Butcher of Lyon," wearing his SS uniform.

"Mr. Wiesel, speaking in a crowded courtroom in tones more sad than angry, said the trial and the testimony of survivors remain in the 'collective consciousness,' helping thereby to prevent the victims of the Nazi genocide from being forgotten."

Another milestone in Elie's quest to ensure that Holocaust victims are never forgotten came in 1993, when the United States Holocaust Memorial Museum opened its doors in Washington, D.C. As the founding chairperson of the U.S. Holocaust Memorial Council and the person who headed the campaign to create the museum, Elie spoke at the dedication ceremony on April 22, 1993.

"A museum is a place, I believe, that should bring people together, a place that should not set people apart," he said in his speech. "To bring the living and the dead together in a spirit of reconciliation [understanding] is part of [my] vision [for this museum]."

U.S. President Bill Clinton and Israeli President Chaim Herzog also spoke on the occasion. Elie's words are carved in stone at the museum's entrance: "For the dead and the living, we must bear witness."

Much Ado about *Night*

By the late 1990s, Elie Wiesel's book *Night*, which had initially been rejected by more than a dozen publishers, was considered one of the most important books ever written about the Holocaust. It had been translated into 30 languages; it had become part of the standard curriculum at high schools and colleges around

LEST WE FORGET

To make sure we learn from—and never forget—the horrors of the Holocaust, about 60 museums and memorials around the world are dedicated to telling the stories of the victims and survivors of this dark period in history.

Most of the world's Holocaust museums are in North America and Europe, but there are a few in other parts of the world, including Japan, Argentina, South Africa, and Russia. The mission statement of the Jewish Holocaust Centre in Melbourne, Australia, sums up the goals of many of the institutions: "We consider the finest memorial to all victims of racist policies to be an educational program which aims to combat anti-Semitism, racism and prejudice in the community and foster understanding between people."

Of the 25 Holocaust museums and memorials in the United States, the largest is the United States Holocaust Memorial Museum in Washington, D.C. Germany is home to seven commemorative venues, including three former concentration camp sites. Four museums are located in Israel, including Yad Vashem Holocaust Martyrs' and Heroes Remembrance Memorial, one of the largest and most significant in the world.

In 1986, Elie Wiesel stands before a photo of a group of inmates, including himself (visible in lower right corner), in Buchenwald in 1945. The photo is part of an exhibit at Yad Vashem, in Jerusalem, Israel. Considered the world's pioneer Holocaust museum, Yad Vashem was conceived in the 1940s, during World War II, in response to reports of the mass murder of Jews in Nazi-occupied Europe. It opened in 1953.

the world; and it was selling about 400,000 copies a year.

As celebrated as *Night* and its author were, they had—and continue to have—their critics. On the extreme side of the political spectrum are Holocaust deniers, who insist the Holocaust never happened and have suggested that Elie made up his story and the historical framework on which it is based.

Despite any criticism or controversy, international respect for Elie Wiesel, his work, and his words has continued to spread.

Some critics who are less extreme in their views have offered more moderate criticism of *Night*. Some scholars say the book tells a good story. They maintain, however, that Elie softened the book from its original Yiddish version to make it appeal to a broader book-buying public.

Others say that it might be more truthfully promoted as an autobiographical novel than a memoir. Others have suggested that Elie is merely a crusader for the Holocaust as "his" cause. These critics feel that he has kept the Holocaust and the suffering of Jews in the public eye. This has had the effect of reducing the significance of other historical genocides.

Elie has also been criticized for supporting Polish American writer Jerzy Kosinski and endorsing Kosinski's *The Painted Bird* (1965). *The Painted Bird* was generally taken to be a semi-autobiographical account based on the author's own experiences during the Holocaust. Years later, the author admitted that the book turned out to be far more fiction than had originally been thought. This and later charges that Kosinski had not actually written the book fueled claims that *The Painted Bird* was a literary hoax.

Into the 21st Century

Despite any criticism or controversy, international respect for Elie Wiesel, his work, and his words has continued to spread—and advancing age hasn't slowed down the contributions of this "teacher, storyteller, and witness," as Elie has called himself.

Top: Romany (Gypsy) prisoners await orders at the Belzec death camp in Nazi-occupied Poland during World War II. Bottom: An Armenian woman kneels before the body of a dead child during World War I. Like the Jews, the Romany people, language, and culture were virtually extinguished in much of Europe by Nazi Germany. Armenians were targets of mass murder and other genocidal practices by the Ottoman (Turkish) Empire.

ELIE WIESEL AND THE DEBATE OVER JERUSALEM

Jerusalem is one of the oldest cities in the world. It contains sites that are holy to Jews, Christians, and Muslims alike.

All of Jerusalem has been under control of the Jewish state of Israel since the 1967 Arab-Israeli War. During that war, Israel captured East Jerusalem from Jordan and annexed it to West Jerusalem, in Israel.

In 1980, Israel declared Jerusalem, including mostly Arab East Jerusalem, the "undivided capital" of Israel. Most of the international community, however, considers Tel Aviv the capital of Israel.

Like others who support keeping all of Jerusalem as part of Israel, Elie Wiesel has said that the city's ties to the Jewish people go far beyond its connection to Christians and Muslims. The idea of a "united" Jerusalem is not accepted by people in the Arab world.

Some criticism has also come from Jews in Israel, Europe, and North America. Many of Elie's critics feel that inflexible attitudes about issues such as Jerusalem are harmful to Israel's overall prospects for peace. These critics also claim that Elie shows a lack of understanding of Middle East politics by suggesting that Jews have a greater religious and historical claim to the entire city of Jerusalem than do other religious and national groups.

In this photo, taken around 1950, Israeli police officers and a Jordanian soldier greet each other across a barbed-wire barrier separating East and West Jerusalem. Israel captured East Jerusalem and other Arab land in 1967. Since then, all of Jerusalem has been under Israeli rule, and the city has remained a point of dispute in the conflict between Arabs and Israelis.

By the end of the 20th century, the 72-year-old had written another 17 books, including a children's book, *King Solomon and His Magic Ring* (1999), and his memoirs in two volumes: *All Rivers Run to the Sea* (1995), and *And the Sea Is Never Full* (1999). He had collected dozens more international honors for his teaching, writing, humanitarian work, and peacemaking—including the U.S. Presidential Medal of Freedom. He had received almost 100 honorary degrees from universities around the world, and he had taken on two more short-term teaching posts—at universities in New York City and St. Petersburg, Florida.

In the early years of the 21st century, Elie was awarded some of the highest honors countries have to offer—the Star of Romania (2002), the Commander's Cross from the Republic of Hungary (2004), the Light of Truth Award from Tibet (2005), and an honorary knighthood from England's Queen Elizabeth II (2006).

In July 2002, the people of Elie's childhood hometown, Sighet, Romania, honored him by turning the house where he was born into a museum that features exhibits about pre-war Jewish life in Sighet. The museum, called the Jewish Culture and Civilization Museum, or the Elie Wiesel Memorial House, is dedicated to the victims of the Holocaust.

"What is abnormal is that I am normal. That I survived the Holocaust and went on to love beautiful girls, to talk, to write, to have toast and tea, and live my life—that is what is abnormal."

Elie Wiesel, 2000

Elie, his wife Marion, his son Shlomo, his sister Hilda, and the Romanian president joined about 5,000 local townspeople at the dedication ceremony. "It was impossible to contain the emotions," said Elie of the event, at which he urged the youth of Sighet to ask their grandparents about that time in spring of 1944 when all their Jewish neighbors vanished.

"Ask them if they shed a tear, if they cried, if they slept well," he said. "And then, when you grow up, tell your children that you have seen a Jew in Sighet telling his story." Today, fewer than 200 Jews live in Sighet.

For years after the war, Elie had been struck by how little his hometown of Sighet, Romania, seemed to have been outwardly affected by the Holocaust. Today, Elie's childhood home is a museum named after him, the person who has become a voice for those most affected by the Holocaust. This plaque, placed on the building, bears the following inscription, written in Romanian and Yiddish: "In this house the writer and professor ELIE WIESEL, Nobel Prize for Peace Laureate in 1986, was born and spent his childhood."

BANDING TOGETHER FOR A CAUSE

In 2006, Elie Wiesel joined forces with one of Hollywood's biggest stars, George Clooney, to bring global attention to the mass killings in the Darfur region of Sudan. The two men met with the United Nations Security Council to ask the organization to send more peacekeeping troops to the African region. By then, more than 200,000 people had been killed in the conflict, which began in 2003.

Elie Wiesel meets with actor George Clooney (left) and Jan Egeland (right), of the United Nations, to discuss bringing relief to Darfur, Sudan.

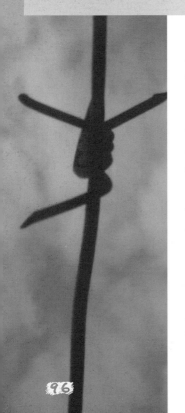

In 2005, another institution took Elie's name when Boston University established the Elie Wiesel Center for Judaic Studies. By then, Elie had been a professor at the university for almost 30 years. The center named for him is a place where scholars focus on Jewish history, culture, and religion.

A year later, Elie made another historical visit into his past. This time, he accompanied world-famous talk show host Oprah Winfrey on an emotional tour of Auschwitz. Their visit was documented in a special, hour-long episode of Oprah's show titled *Oprah And Elie Wiesel at the Auschwitz Death Camp*. It aired May 24, 2006.

THE OPRAH EFFECT

In May 2011, talk show host Oprah Winfrey signed off from her daily talk show for the last time. By then, after 25 years on the air, she had become one of the most influential people in the world. Any product she promoted on the *Oprah Winfrey Show* became an instant must-have item. Some companies saw their sales multiply by a factor of 100. That means, if the company usually sold ten units of the featured product in a day, it was suddenly selling 1,000 a day after Oprah got her hands on it. That sales boost was called "The Oprah Effect," and it affected the books she selected for her monthly book club in the same way—as Elie discovered in 2006.

After Oprah chose *Night* for her book club in January 2006, it sold three million copies in 18 months. Prior to that, *Night* had sold seven million copies in 46 years. The book spent the next 80 weeks—that's more than a year and a half— on the *New York Times* Bestseller List because of Oprah's influence. At that point, the *Times* decided *Night* belonged on a classic book list, rather than on the list reserved for new releases, and removed it.

Oprah Winfrey and Elie Wiesel at the 2007 Elie Wiesel Foundation for Humanity dinner in New York. Oprah was given the Foundation's Humanitarian Award for her efforts to positively affect the lives of people all over the world, particularly children.

Setbacks

Amid all the honors, attention, and other positive events in Elie's life, he has also suffered some serious setbacks in recent years. In 2007, a Holocaust denier named Eric Hunt attacked Elie in a San Francisco hotel, where Elie was attending a peace conference. The young man got into the elevator with Elie and said he wanted to interview him. Elie suggested they talk in the lobby, but when the elevator opened at the sixth floor, Hunt tried to drag the 79-year-old into a hotel room. The young man fled when Elie started yelling for help.

Hunt later bragged about the attempted abduction on a Holocaust-denier website: "I had planned to bring Wiesel to my hotel room where he would truthfully answer my questions regarding the fact that his non-fiction Holocaust memoir, *Night*, is almost entirely fictitious."

The 22-year-old was arrested two weeks later at a substance abuse clinic in New Jersey, where he was a patient. He was convicted, sentenced to two years in prison for his hate crime, and ordered to take psychological treatment. "Crimes motivated by hate are among the most reprehensible of offenses," said San Francisco District Attorney Kamala Harris. "This defendant has been made to answer for an unwarranted and biased attack on a man who has dedicated his life to peace." At his sentencing hearing, Eric said he no longer denied the Holocaust. He continues, however, to maintain a Holocaust-denier website.

In late 2008, Elie and the foundation that bears his name suffered a huge blow when investment manager Bernard ("Bernie") Madoff was arrested for committing the largest investment fraud in history. Madoff was later found guilty of swindling thousands of people and organizations out of billions of dollars over a period of at least 20 years.

The Elie Wiesel Foundation for Humanity was one of Madoff's victims. The organization estimated its loss at $15.2 million—virtually everything it had. Elie and Marion also lost their life savings to this "thief, scoundrel, criminal," as Elie called Madoff. "I am not a genius of finance. I teach philosophy and literature—and so it happened," said Elie.

Toward the end of 2009, about a year after Madoff was arrested, the Elie Wiesel Foundation posted this note on its website:

> *"Thanks to generosity from around the country and world, with donations from $5 and up, we are pleased to let you know that we are able to honor all of our commitments and continue all of our projects."*

The organization would recover.

Into Tomorrow

As the first decade of the 21st century wound down, Elie, now in his 80s, barely slowed his pace. He wrote another ten books, making a career total of more than 50. That works out to a book a year since *Night* was published in 1960. He continued to earn honorary doctorates, literary awards, and international honors. He continued to lecture at conferences around the world. He also continued to speak out against persecution and oppression everywhere.

Bernie Madoff, whose investment fraud bilked thousands of people and groups out of billions of dollars, was sentenced to 150 years in prison for his crimes. One of the organizations victimized by Madoff was the Elie Wiesel Foundation for Humanity.

No Part in This Play

In 2010, a play called *Imagining Madoff* was to make its theater debut in Washington, D.C. The play featured an imaginary confrontation between a character named Elie Wiesel and the man who nearly ruined him—financier Bernie Madoff. Before the play's scheduled premiere, though, the real Elie heard about it and threatened to sue the woman who wrote the play, Deborah Margolin. She ended up changing the Wiesel character's name to Solomon Galkin, and the revised play made its debut in Hudson, New York, in the summer of 2010.

In 2003, Elie led the International Commission for the Study of the Holocaust in Romania. The organization came to be called the Wiesel Commission in honor of his leadership. He joined the International Council of the Human Rights Foundation, which was created in 2005. In 2009, he accompanied U.S. President Barack Obama on a visit to Buchenwald, where Elie's father had died 64 years earlier.

For President Obama, the former concentration camp was one stop on a six-day political tour of Europe. For Elie, the trip to Buchenwald was "a way of coming [to] visit my father's grave—but he had no grave."

Elie spoke without notes and with such heartfelt sentiment that even the members of the media were moved by "the powerful eloquence of his words," as one *Time* magazine writer said.

During this visit, Elie addressed the guilt he still felt over ignoring the dying cries of his father all those years ago:

"The day he died was one of the darkest in my life. He became sick, weak, and I was there. I was there when he suffered. I was there when he asked for help, for water. I was there to receive his last words. But I was not there when he called for me, although we were in the same block; he on the upper bed and I on the lower bed. He called my name, and I was too afraid to move. All of us were. And then he died. I was there, but I was not there.

"And I thought, one day I will come back and speak to him, and tell him of the world that has become mine.... Thank you, Mr. President, for allowing me to come back to my father's grave, which is still in my heart."

The Legacy of Elie Wiesel

It has been more than 65 years since he walked out of Buchenwald, and still, Elie Wiesel has no idea why his life was spared. He rejects the suggestion that he was chosen by God to survive to bear witness, to speak up for those who died. "I have no explanation [for my survival]," he once told talk show host Oprah Winfrey. "Believe me, I have tried to know, but I do not. If it is God, I have problems with that. If he bothered to save me, why couldn't he have saved all the others? There were people worthier than I."

Elie did survive, and because he did, he said, "I must do everything possible to help others." That has meant a lifetime of writing, educating, and speaking out about global injustices. In the 50-plus years since he wrote *Night*, Elie has been called "the voice for the

voiceless," "the spiritual archivist of the Holocaust," "a witness for truth and justice," and "one of our most important spiritual leaders and guides." And still, he doesn't rest.

In late 2009, Elie made a speech to 10,000 people attending an anti-racist gathering in Hungary. It was his first visit to that country since the Holocaust. In 2010, President Barack Obama awarded Elie the National Humanities Medal. A few months later, Elie and the president met at the White House to discuss peace in the Middle East. In 2011, Elie spoke at commencement ceremonies at Washington University in St. Louis, Missouri, where he was awarded another honorary degree.

In June 2009, Elie Wiesel accompanied U.S. President Barack Obama on a visit to Buchenwald. Here, they are joined at the former concentration camp by German Chancellor Angela Merkel.

Perhaps Elie continues to work at this frantic pace to "fulfill his obligation to the dead, and thus justify his survival," as one essayist has suggested. Or perhaps it's because he remembers being a child, a 15-year-old who was taken from his mother, a teenager who helplessly watched babies die in a pit of fire, a young man who couldn't save his father from beatings and death. Perhaps it's because he remembers that, as all this happened, the world remained silent—nobody came to help Elie and his family. Perhaps it's because, even today,

Elie Wiesel cannot remain silent in the face of suffering in the world.

"If I could bring back one child, I would give up anything I have," said Elie in a 1996 interview. "If I could...free one prisoner, I would give up a lot. If I could give a feeling of solidarity to a person who is abandoned, I would still give a lot. I would like to do things I cannot do. All I have is a few words, and I will give these words. That's what I'm trying to do."

Chronology

September 30, 1928 Eliezer ("Elie") Wiesel is born in Sighet, Romania.

January 1933 Adolf Hitler and his Nazi Party take power in Germany.

1939 Hitler announces his plan to kill all Jews.

September 1, 1939 Germany invades Poland; World War II begins.

May 1940 Auschwitz opens.

September 1941 Nazis experiment with gas chambers; 850 people are gassed to death at Auschwitz.

December 7, 1941 Japan bombs Pearl Harbor; U.S. enters WWII.

April–May 1944 Nazis arrest Jewish leaders and close synagogues in Sighet. Jews are confined to ghettos behind barbed wire. All Jews are deported from Sighet. The day his family arrives at Auschwitz is the last day Elie sees his mother and little sister; later that day, Elie is tattooed with the identity number A-7713.

June 1944 Elie and his father, Shlomo, are transferred to Buna, the largest Auschwitz work camp.

January 1945 Elie undergoes surgery on infected foot; he and Shlomo join an evacuation march from Auschwitz to Buchenwald. On January 28, Shlomo dies.

April 1945 Buchenwald is liberated. On April 30, Adolf Hitler and his wife, Eva Braun, commit suicide.

May 1945 Elie is among hundreds of orphaned Jewish children sent to France to start new lives; eventually, he is reunited with his two older sisters. On May 7, Germany surrenders; WWII is over in Europe.

August 1945 U.S. drops two atomic bombs on Japan; Japan surrenders; WWII is over in the Pacific.

1948 Elie enrolls at the Sorbonne.

1949 Elie begins journalism career, writing for a French newspaper; later works as Paris correspondent for an Israeli newspaper.

1952 Elie quits the Sorbonne, becomes a full-time journalist.

1956 Elie moves to New York to become a U.S. correspondent for an Israeli newspaper; he is hit by a taxicab, seriously injured, and confined to a wheelchair for a year.

1960 *Night* is published.

1963 Elie becomes a U.S. citizen.

1969 Elie marries Marion Erster Rose; three years later, their son Shlomo Elisha is born.

1972 Elie begins teaching at City University of New York.

1976 Elie begins teaching at Boston University.

1978 U.S. President Carter appoints Elie Chairman of President's Commission on the Holocaust.

1985 U.S. President Reagan presents Elie with the U.S. Congressional Gold Medal of Achievement; in his acceptance speech, Elie begs the President to cancel an upcoming trip to a German military cemetery.

December 10, 1986 Elie is awarded the Nobel Peace Prize.

1987 Elie and Marion establish Elie Wiesel Foundation for Humanity. Elie later testifies at the trial of war criminal Klaus Barbie.

2002 Elie's Sighet, Romania, home becomes the Jewish Culture and Civilization Museum, or Elie Wiesel Memorial House.

2005 Boston University establishes the Elie Wiesel Center for Judaic Studies.

January 2006 Elie's *Night* is the selection-of-the-month for Oprah Winfrey's Book Club; later this year, Oprah and Elie visit Auschwitz together; their visit is the subject of a special episode of Oprah's show.

2007 Elie is attacked in San Francisco by a Holocaust denier.

2009 Elie accompanies U.S. President Obama on a visit to Buchenwald.

2010 President Obama awards Elie the National Humanities Medal.

Glossary

activist One who believes in a cause and takes action to promote that belief

Allies The countries that fought in World War II against Nazi Germany-for example, the United States and Canada

annex To add as an extra part; to add land to one's own territory

atomic bomb A bomb of great power; the bomb's explosive energy comes from a chemical reaction involving splitting atoms

atrocity An act of extreme cruelty

autobiography A life story as written by the person who has lived that story; a story about oneself

Axis The countries that fought in WWII on the side of Nazi Germany—for example, Japan and Italy

beadle A person who helps in a church or synagogue by doing tasks such as cleaning, office work, or ushering people to their seats

concentration camp A place where political prisoners or others considered undesirable or enemies of the state are housed, usually under dreadful conditions

crematorium A furnace for cremating, or burning, dead bodies

curriculum A group of courses that make up an educational program

defendant The person or group accused or sued in a court of law

dehumanize To make people stop feeling and acting like humans by depriving them of kindness, compassion, personal power, and other positive qualities of life

deportation Sending an person or a group of people out of a country where they have no rights

doctoral dissertation A lengthy academic research paper; required for earning a PhD degree

dysentery A painful intestinal illness that usually results in vomiting and/or diarrhea

exile The state of being banned or expelled from one's native land, usually for political reasons or as a form of punishment

extermination Complete destruction; the goal of the Nazis in World War II was the extermination of European Jews

genocide The deliberate killing of a group of people, especially those of a particular ethnic group, religion, or belief system

Gestapo Brutal, secret state police in Nazi Germany

ghetto An area where people of similar backgrounds live together, usually in poor conditions

Hasidic Jew A member of a branch of Orthodox Judaism that is based on ideas involving an intense, often mystical, connection between Jews and their God

Holocaust denier A person who does not believe that the Holocaust happened or, if it did, that it wasn't as terrible as the historical evidence shows

honorary Given or granted as an honor, without having to fulfill usual requirements; symbolic

humanitarian A person devoted to helping others, relieving suffering of others, and improving the lives of others

infirmary A small hospital, or a room within a building that serves as a medical facility

Kaddish Jewish prayer for the dead

kapo A privileged prisoner who served as a barracks supervisor/warder or led work details in a Nazi concentration camp

legitimate Allowable, acceptable, lawful, or conforming to rules

Nazi Party Short for the National Socialist German Workers Party; the party controlled by Hitler

oppression Unjust or cruel control of a person or group of people by those in a position of power

rabbi A Jewish spiritual leader

resistance movement Organized groups that worked in secret to help the Allies in their fight against the Nazis during WWII

Rosh Hashanah The Jewish New Year and first of the Jewish High Holy Days, which occur in autumn

secular Non-religious

shtetl A small Jewish town or village in Eastern Europe

spectrum A range of choices or possibilities on which a person or group may be placed

SS Short for *Schutzstaffel,* which means "protection squadron"; founded as a bodyguard service for Adolf Hitler, it grew into a brutal police force of 250,000 members by the time World War II started in 1939

synagogue A Jewish place of religious worship

Talmud A body of texts explaining the meaning behind the laws, customs, and beliefs of the Jewish religion

Torah The first five books of the Jewish Scriptures, or Hebrew Bible; also known as The Five Books of Moses, the Torah is the most holy text in Judaism

Yeshiva an Orthodox Jewish school

Yiddish A language primarily spoken by Jews of Central and Eastern European background

Further Information

Books

Adams, Simon. *Eyewitness World War II.* New York: Dorling Kindersley, 2009.

Koestler-Grack, Rachel A. *Elie Wiesel: Witness for Humanity*.
New York: Gareth Stevens, 2009.

Rosenberg, Aaron. *World War II Profiles*. New York: Scholastic, 2011.

Wiesel, Elie. *Night* (with a new translation by Marion Wiesel).
New York: Hill and Wang, 2006.

Websites

www.jewishvirtuallibrary.org/index.html
The Jewish Virtual Library is the most comprehensive online Jewish
encyclopedia in the world. Divided into 13 sections, it features thousands of
articles and photographs. Elie Wiesel's biography is in the Biographies section
at *http://www.jewishvirtuallibrary.org/jsource/biography/Wiesel.html*

www.ushmm.org/
The United States Holocaust Memorial Museum site is an amazing resource
for information about anything related to the Holocaust. It has a fantastic
Learning Site for Students at *http://www.ushmm.org/outreach/en/*
It also has an excellent section devoted to Elie Wiesel, with dozens of related
links, photos, and maps at
http://www.ushmm.org/wlc/en/article.php?ModuleId=10007176

www.oprah.com/oprahsbookclub/Your-Guide-to-Night-and-Elie-Wiesel/1
"Your Guide to *Night*" on Oprah's Book Club site includes an excerpt from
Elie Wiesel's *Night,* a biography of Elie, glossary of terms related to the book,
reading guides, and links to related resources.

http://en.auschwitz.org.pl/h/
This is the home page for the History section of the Auschwitz-Birkenau Memorial and Museum site. From here, you can navigate to articles about the building of Auschwitz, prisoners' life at the camp, experiences of children there, and many other subjects. On the Visiting Auschwitz section of the site, you can take a virtual tour of the Memorial and Museum in Poland: *http://en.auschwitz.org.pl/z/index.php?option=com_content&task=view&id=6&Itemid=8*

www.eliewieselfoundation.org/
This is the Elie Wiesel Foundation for Humanity site. Here, you will find a biography of Elie, a listing of all his books, and information about the foundation he and his wife, Marion, started in 1987.

Video

First Person Singular: Elie Wiesel (a PBS DVD/video). Lives and Legacies Films, Inc., 2002.

We Day: Elie Wiesel on Hope, Compassion, and the Power of Youth. Free the Children, 2009.
Elie Wiesel's speech to 16,000 young people at We Day in Toronto, Ontario, Canada, on Oct. 5, 2009. Find this video at *www.weday.com/learn/videos/keLT6bp7wok*

Oprah and Elie Wiesel at Auschwitz Death Camp. Harpo, Inc., 2006.
Oprah's special episode documenting her visit to Auschwitz with Elie Wiesel. On YouTube in six parts:
Part 1: www.youtube.com/watch?v=slZMOkYJFO0
Part 2: www.youtube.com/watch?v=mUEEYa0pvgU&feature=related
Part 3: www.youtube.com/watch?v=LoRfhm48b-0&feature=related
Part 4: www.youtube.com/watch?v=kXP2L3MG7gs&feature=related
Part 5: www.youtube.com/watch?v=X6hyhxUWb1k&feature=related
Part 6: www.youtube.com/watch?v=4-xm6nUbeXQ&feature=fvwrel

Index

Index

About the Author

Diane Dakers was born and raised in Toronto, and now divides her time between Victoria, British Columbia, and Ottawa, Ontario, where she is working on a Master of Journalism degree. A specialist in Canadian arts and cultural issues, Diane has been a newspaper, magazine, television, and radio journalist since 1991. She loves finding and telling stories about what makes people tick—be they world changers like Elie Wiesel or lesser-known folks like you and me.